THE
INFLUENCE
OF
DARWIN
ON
PHILOSOPHY
AND OTHER ESSAYS

THE
INFLUENCE
OF
DARWIN
ON
PHILOSOPHY
AND OTHER ESSAYS

JOHN
DEWEY

GREAT BOOKS IN PHILOSOPHY

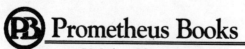 **Prometheus Books**

59 John Glenn Drive
Amherst, New York 14228-2197

Published 1997 by Prometheus Books

59 John Glenn Drive, Amherst, New York 14228–2197,
716–691–0133. FAX: 716–691–0137.

Library of Congress Cataloging-in-Publication Data

Dewey, John, 1859–1952.
    The influence of Darwin on philosophy and other essays / John
Dewey.
        p.   cm. — (Great books in philosophy)
    Originally published: New York : H. Holt and Co., 1910.
    Includes bibliographical references and index.
    ISBN 1–57392–137–8 (pbk. : alk. paper)
    1. Evolution. 2. Pragmatism. I. Title. II. Series.
B945.D43I4   1997
191—dc21   97–4502
                                                              CIP

Printed in the United States of America on acid-free paper.

Additional Titles on Metaphysics and Epistemology in Prometheus's Great Books in Philosophy Series

See the back of this volume for a complete list of titles in
Prometheus's Great Books in Philosophy and Great Minds series.

JOHN DEWEY was born near Burlington, Vermont, on October 20, 1859. Twenty years later, he graduated from the University of Vermont, after which he taught public school in Pennsylvania and Vermont. Having become interested in philosophical questions while still an undergraduate, Dewey continued his philosophical training at Johns Hopkins University. In 1884 he was awarded a doctorate in philosophy from that institution and soon thereafter he accepted a position in philosophy at the University of Michigan. Except for a one-year appointment as professor of philosophy at the University of Minnesota, Dewey remained at Michigan—serving a five-year term as chairman—until 1894 when he moved with his wife, Alice Chipman, to the University of Chicago and began his tenure as chairman of the philosophy department. It was at Chicago that Dewey received national recognition for his pioneering work in the field of education with the development of his laboratory school in which experimental approaches to teaching were explored. After a falling out with the University of Chicago over the administration of the school, Dewey left in 1904 and accepted a professorship in philosophy at Columbia University.

For the next twenty-six years, Dewey's academic position at Columbia served as a springboard for his many and varied interests, e.g., social questions, politics, education, and public affairs. As Dewey's national and international reputation grew, he began working with such groups as the American Philosophical Association, the American Association of University Professors (founder and first president), the Teacher's Union, and the American Civil Liberties Union, among others.

Unlike those who consider retirement a time to relax and enjoy the restful pleasures of later life, John Dewey dedicated his remaining years to sorting out the tough social questions facing America and the world. He joined organizations whose goal was to increase public education in the areas of domestic and international politics. One of Dewey's most famous public forums was his participation in the commission that met in Mexico City to inquire into the charges leveled against Leon Trotsky at his Moscow trial. The commission subsequently found Trotsky innocent of the charges. Dewey was also one of several colleagues who publicly defended fellow philosopher Bertrand Russell when Russell was denied a teaching position at the City College of New York because of public criticism of his views on marriage and religion.

In developing his own unique philosophical stance, John Dewey overcame Hegelian idealism to embrace the pragmatic views of William James. Dewey's devotion to free inquiry and the scientific method found him spearheading the intellectual opposition against the belief that absolute knowledge can be attained in a world of variegated circumstances, discoveries, trailblazing research, and advances of all kinds. For Dewey, knowledge is not absolute, immutable, and eternal, but rather relative to the developmental interaction of man with his world as problems arise to present themselves for solution. This scientific approach, which allows one to declare the truth of a claim until—and only until—there is negative evidence sufficient to disconfirm the hypothesis, opens the mind to the need for a democratic approach to problem solving. Without cooperation and a rational tolerance for diverse points of view within a pluralistic community, society has no hope of mature development.

During his ninety-three years, John Dewey authored more than two dozen books and scores of articles in both scholarly and popular publications. He is truly America's foremost philosopher, whose work will influence intellectuals throughout the world for many years to come.

John Dewey died in New York City on June 1, 1952.

PREFACE

An elaborate preface to a philosophic work usually impresses one as a last desperate effort on the part of its author to convey what he feels he has not quite managed to say in the body of his book. Nevertheless, a collection of essays on various topics written during a series of years may perhaps find room for an independent word to indicate the kind of unity they seem, to their writer, to possess. Probably every one acquainted with present philosophic thought—found, with some notable exceptions, in periodicals rather than in books—would term it a philosophy of transition and reconstruction. Its various representatives agree in what they oppose—the orthodox British empiricism of two generations ago and the orthodox Neo-Kantian idealism of the last generation—rather than in what they proffer.

The essays of this volume belong, I suppose, to what has come to be known (since the earlier of them were written) as the pragmatic phase of the newer movement. Now a recent German critic has described pragmatism as, " Epistemologically, nominalism; psychologically, voluntarism; cosmologically, energism; metaphysically, agnosticism; ethically, meliorism on the basis of the Bentham-

Mill utilitarianism." [1] It may be that pragmatism
will turn out to be all of this formidable array;
but even should it, the one who thus defines it has
hardly come within earshot of it. For whatever
else pragmatism is or is not, the pragmatic spirit
is primarily a revolt against that habit of mind
which disposes of anything whatever—even so
humble an affair as a new method in Philosophy—
by tucking it away, after this fashion, in the
pigeon holes of a filing cabinet. There are other
vital phases of contemporary transition and revision; there are, for example, a new realism and
naturalistic idealism. When I recall that I find
myself more interested (even though their representatives might decline to reciprocate) in such
phases than in the systems marked by the labels
of our German critic, I am confirmed in a belief
that after all it is better to view pragmatism quite
vaguely as part and parcel of a general movement of intellectual reconstruction. For otherwise we seem to have no recourse save to define
pragmatism—as does our German author—in
terms of the very past systems against which it is
a reaction; or, in escaping that alternative, to regard it as a fixed rival system making like claim to

[1] The affair is even more portentous in the German with
its capital letters and series of *muses:* "Gewiss ist der
Pragmatismus erkenntnisstheoretisch Nominalismus, psy-
chologisch Voluntarismus, naturphilosophisch Energismus,
metaphysisch Agnosticismus, ethisch Meliorismus auf
Grundlage des Bentham-Millschen Utilitarismus."

completeness and finality. And if, as I believe, one of the marked traits of the pragmatic movement is just the surrender of every such claim, how have we furthered our understanding of pragmatism?

Classic philosophies have to be revised because they must be squared up with the many social and intellectual tendencies that have revealed themselves since those philosophies matured. The conquest of the sciences by the experimental method of inquiry; the injection of evolutionary ideas into the study of life and society; the application of the historic method to religions and morals as well as to institutions; the creation of the sciences of " origins " and of the cultural development of mankind—how can such intellectual changes occur and leave philosophy what it was and where it was? Nor can philosophy remain an indifferent spectator of the rise of what may be termed the new individualism in art and letters, with its naturalistic method applied in a religious, almost mystic spirit to what is primitive, obscure, varied, inchoate, and growing in nature and human character. The age of Darwin, Helmholtz, Pasteur, Ibsen, Maeterlinck, Rodin, and Henry James must feel some uneasiness until it has liquidated its philosophic inheritance in current intellectual coin. And to accuse those who are concerned in this transaction of ignorant contempt for the classic past of philosophy is to overlook the inspiration the movement of translation draws from the fact that the history of philosophy has become only too well understood.

Any revision of customary notions with its elimination—instead of " solution "—of many traditionary problems cannot hope, however, for any unity save that of tendency and operation. Elaborate and imposing system, the regimenting and uniforming of thoughts, are, at present, evidence that we are assisting at a stage performance in which borrowed—or hired—figures are maneuvering. Tentatively and piecemeal must the reconstruction of our stock notions proceed. As a contribution to such a revision, the present collection of essays is submitted. With one or two exceptions, their order is that of a reversed chronology, the later essays coming first. The facts regarding the conditions of their first appearance are given in connection with each essay. I wish to thank the Editors of the *Philosophical Review*, of *Mind*, of the *Hibbert Journal*, of the *Journal of Philosophy, Psychology, and Scientific Methods*, and of the *Popular Science Monthly*, and the Directors of the Press of Chicago and Columbia Universities, respectively, for permission to reprint such of the essays as appeared originally under their several auspices.

JOHN DEWEY

COLUMBIA UNIVERSITY,
NEW YORK CITY, March 1, 1910.

CONTENTS

THE INFLUENCE OF DARWINISM ON PHILOSOPHY [1]

I

THAT the publication of the "Origin of Species" marked an epoch in the development of the natural sciences is well known to the layman. That the combination of the very words origin and species embodied an intellectual revolt and introduced a new intellectual temper is easily overlooked by the expert. The conceptions that had reigned in the philosophy of nature and knowledge for two thousand years, the conceptions that had become the familiar furniture of the mind, rested on the assumption of the superiority of the fixed and final; they rested upon treating change and origin as signs of defect and unreality. In laying hands upon the sacred ark of absolute permanency, in treating the forms that had been regarded as types of fixity and perfection as

[1] A lecture in a course of public lectures on "Charles Darwin and His Influence on Science," given at Columbia University in the winter and spring of 1909. Reprinted from the *Popular Science Monthly* for July, 1909.

originating and passing away, the "Origin of Species" introduced a mode of thinking that in the end was bound to transform the logic of knowledge, and hence the treatment of morals, politics, and religion.

No wonder, then, that the publication of Darwin's book, a half century ago, precipitated a crisis. The true nature of the controversy is easily concealed from us, however, by the theological clamor that attended it. The vivid and popular features of the anti-Darwinian row tended to leave the impression that the issue was between science on one side and theology on the other. Such was not the case—the issue lay primarily within science itself, as Darwin himself early recognized. The theological outcry he discounted from the start, hardly noticing it save as it bore upon the " feelings of his female relatives." But for two decades before final publication he contemplated the possibility of being put down by his scientific peers as a fool or as crazy; and he set, as the measure of his success, the degree in which he should affect three men of science: Lyell in geology, Hooker in botany, and Huxley in zoology.

Religious considerations lent fervor to the controversy, but they did not provoke it. Intellectually, religious emotions are not creative but conservative. They attach themselves readily to the current view of the world and consecrate it. They

steep and dye intellectual fabrics in the seething
vat of emotions; they do not form their warp
and woof.   There is not, I think, an instance of
any large idea about the world being independently
generated by religion.   Although the ideas that
rose up like armed men against Darwinism owed
their intensity to religious associations, their origin
and meaning are to be sought in science and philosophy, not in religion.

II

Few words in our language foreshorten intellectual history as much as does the word species.
The Greeks, in initiating the intellectual life of
Europe, were impressed by characteristic traits
of the life of plants and animals; so impressed
indeed that they made these traits the key to
defining nature and to explaining mind and society.
And truly, life is so wonderful that a seemingly
successful reading of its mystery might well lead
men to believe that the key to the secrets of
heaven and earth was in their hands.   The Greek
rendering of this mystery, the Greek formulation
of the aim and standard of knowledge, was in the
course of time embodied in the word species, and it
controlled philosophy for two thousand years.   To
understand the intellectual face-about expressed
in the phrase " Origin of Species," we must, then,

understand the long dominant idea against which it
is a protest.

Consider how men were impressed by the facts
of life. Their eyes fell upon certain things slight
in bulk, and frail in structure. To every appearance, these perceived things were inert and passive.
Suddenly, under certain circumstances, these
things—henceforth known as seeds or eggs or
germs—begin to change, to change rapidly in size,
form, and qualities. Rapid and extensive changes
occur, however, in many things—as when wood is
touched by fire. But the changes in the living
thing are orderly; they are cumulative; they tend
constantly in one direction; they do not, like other
changes, destroy or consume, or pass fruitless into
wandering flux; they realize and fulfil. Each successive stage, no matter how unlike its predecessor,
preserves its net effect and also prepares the way
for a fuller activity on the part of its successor. In
living beings, changes do not happen as they seem
to happen elsewhere, any which way; the earlier
changes are regulated in view of later results.
This progressive organization does not cease till
there is achieved a true final term, a $\tau \epsilon \lambda \acute{o} \varsigma$, a completed, perfected end. This final form exercises
in turn a plenitude of functions, not the least note-
worthy of which is production of germs like those
from which it took its own origin, germs capable
of the same cycle of self-fulfilling activity.

But the whole miraculous tale is not yet told. The same drama is enacted to the same destiny in countless myriads of individuals so sundered in time, so severed in space, that they have no opportunity for mutual consultation and no means of interaction. As an old writer quaintly said, "things of the same kind go through the same formalities"—celebrate, as it were, the same ceremonial rites.

This formal activity which operates throughout a series of changes and holds them to a single course; which subordinates their aimless flux to its own perfect manifestation; which, leaping the boundaries of space and time, keeps individuals distant in space and remote in time to a uniform type of structure and function: this principle seemed to give insight into the very nature of reality itself. To it Aristotle gave the name, εἶδος. This term the scholastics translated as *species*.

The force of this term was deepened by its application to everything in the universe that observes order in flux and manifests constancy through change. From the casual drift of daily weather, through the uneven recurrence of seasons and unequal return of seed time and harvest, up to the majestic sweep of the heavens—the image of eternity in time—and from this to the unchanging pure and contemplative intelligence beyond nature lies one unbroken fulfilment of ends. Nature as a whole is a progressive realization of purpose strictly comparable to the realization of purpose in any single plant or animal.

The conception of εἶδος, species, a fixed form and final cause, was the central principle of knowledge as well as of nature. Upon it rested the logic of science. Change as change is mere flux and lapse; it insults intelligence. Genuinely to know is to grasp a permanent end that realizes itself through changes, holding them thereby within the metes and bounds of fixed truth. Completely to know is to relate all special forms to their one single end and good: pure contemplative intelligence. Since, however, the scene of nature which directly confronts us is in change, nature as directly and practically experienced does not satisfy the conditions of knowledge. Human experience is in flux, and hence the instrumentalities of sense-perception and of inference based upon observation are condemned in advance. Science is compelled to aim at realities lying behind and beyond the processes of nature, and to carry on its search for these realities by means of rational forms transcending ordinary modes of perception and inference.

There are, indeed, but two alternative courses. We must either find the appropriate objects and organs of knowledge in the mutual interactions of changing things; or else, to escape the infection of change, we *must* seek them in some transcendent and supernal region. The human mind, deliberately as it were, exhausted the logic of the changeless, the final, and the transcendent, before it essayed adventure on the pathless wastes of generation and transformation. We dispose all too easily of the efforts of the schoolmen to interpret nature and mind in terms of real essences, hidden forms, and occult faculties, forgetful of the seriousness and dignity of the ideas that lay behind. We dispose of them by laughing at the famous gentleman who accounted for the fact that opium put people to sleep on the ground it had a dormitive faculty. But the doctrine, held in our own day, that knowledge of the plant that yields the poppy consists in referring the peculiarities of an individual to a type, to a universal form, a doctrine so firmly established that any other method of knowing was conceived to be unphilosophical and unscientific, is a survival of precisely the same logic. This identity of conception in the scholastic and anti-Darwinian theory may well suggest greater sympathy for what has become unfamiliar as well as greater humility regarding the further unfamiliarities that history has in store.

Darwin was not, of course, the first to question the classic philosophy of nature and of knowledge. The beginnings of the revolution are in the physical science of the sixteenth and seventeenth centuries. When Galileo said: " It is my opinion that the earth is very noble and admirable by reason of so many and so different alterations and generations which are incessantly made therein," he expressed the changed temper that was coming over the world; the transfer of interest from the permanent to the changing. When Descartes said: " The nature of physical things is much more easily conceived when they are beheld coming gradually into existence, than when they are only considered as produced at once in a finished and perfect state," the modern world became self-conscious of the logic that was henceforth to control it, the logic of which Darwin's " Origin of Species " is the latest scientific achievement. Without the methods of Copernicus, Kepler, Galileo, and their successors in astronomy, physics, and chemistry, Darwin would have been helpless in the organic sciences. But prior to Darwin the impact of the new scientific method upon life, mind, and politics, had been arrested, because between these ideal or moral interests and the inorganic world intervened the kingdom of plants and animals. The gates of the garden of life were barred to the new ideas; and only through this garden was there access to mind and politics. The influence of Darwin upon philosophy resides in his having conquered the phenomena of life for the principle of transition, and thereby freed the new logic for application to mind and morals and life. When he said of species what Galileo had said of the earth, *e pur se muove*, he emancipated, once for all, genetic and experimental ideas as an organon of asking questions and looking for explanations.

III

The exact bearings upon philosophy of the new logical outlook are, of course, as yet, uncertain and inchoate. We live in the twilight of intellectual transition. One must add the rashness of the prophet to the stubbornness of the partizan to venture a systematic exposition of the influence upon philosophy of the Darwinian method. At best, we can but inquire as to its general bearing—the effect upon mental temper and complexion, upon that body of half-conscious, half-instinctive intellectual aversions and preferences which determine, after all, our more deliberate intellectual enterprises. In this vague inquiry there happens to exist as a kind of touchstone a problem of long historic currency that has also been much discussed in Darwinian literature. I refer to the old problem of design *versus* chance, mind *versus* matter, as the causal explanation, first or final, of things.

As we have already seen, the classic notion of

species carried with it the idea of purpose. In all living forms, a specific type is present directing the earlier stages of growth to the realization of its own perfection. Since this purposive regulative principle is not visible to the senses, it follows that it must be an ideal or rational force. Since, however, the perfect form is gradually approximated through the sensible changes, it also follows that in and through a sensible realm a rational ideal force is working out its own ultimate manifestation. These inferences were extended to nature: (*a*) She does nothing in vain; but all for an ulterior purpose. (*b*) Within natural sensible events there is therefore contained a spiritual causal force, which as spiritual escapes perception, but is apprehended by an enlightened reason. (*c*) The manifestation of this principle brings about a subordination of matter and sense to its own realization, and this ultimate fulfilment is the goal of nature and of man. The design argument thus operated in two directions. Purposefulness accounted for the intelligibility of nature and the possibility of science, while the absolute or cosmic character of this purposefulness gave sanction and worth to the moral and religious endeavors of man. Science was underpinned and morals authorized by one and the same principle, and their mutual agreement was eternally guaranteed.

This philosophy remained, in spite of sceptical and polemic outbursts, the official and the regnant philosophy of Europe for over two thousand years. The expulsion of fixed first and final causes from astronomy, physics, and chemistry had indeed given the doctrine something of a shock. But, on the other hand, increased acquaintance with the details of plant and animal life operated as a counterbalance and perhaps even strengthened the argument from design. The marvelous adaptations of organisms to their environment, of organs to the organism, of unlike parts of a complex organ—like the eye—to the organ itself; the foreshadowing by lower forms of the higher; the preparation in earlier stages of growth for organs that only later had their functioning—these things were increasingly recognized with the progress of botany, zoology, paleontology, and embryology. Together, they added such prestige to the design argument that by the late eighteenth century it was, as approved by the sciences of organic life, the central point of theistic and idealistic philosophy.

The Darwinian principle of natural selection cut straight under this philosophy. If all organic adaptations are due simply to constant variation and the elimination of those variations which are harmful in the struggle for existence that is brought about by excessive reproduction, there is no call for a prior intelligent causal force to plan and preordain them. Hostile critics charged Darwin with materialism and with making chance the cause of the universe.

Some naturalists, like Asa Gray, favored the Darwinian principle and attempted to reconcile it with design. Gray held to what may be called design on the installment plan. If we conceive the " stream of variations " to be itself intended, we may suppose that each successive variation was designed from the first to be selected. In that case, variation, struggle, and selection simply define the mechanism of " secondary causes " through which the " first cause " acts; and the doctrine of design is none the worse off because we know more of its *modus operandi*.

Darwin could not accept this mediating proposal. He admits or rather he asserts that it is " impossible to conceive this immense and wonderful universe including man with his capacity of looking far backwards and far into futurity as the result of blind chance or necessity." [1] But nevertheless he holds that since variations are in useless as well as useful directions, and since the latter are sifted out simply by the stress of the conditions of struggle for existence, the design argument as applied to living beings is unjustifiable; and its lack of support there deprives it

[1] "Life and Letters," Vol. I., p. 282; cf. 285.

of scientific value as applied to nature in general.
If the variations of the pigeon, which under artificial selection give the pouter pigeon, are not preordained for the sake of the breeder, by what logic
do we argue that variations resulting in natural
species are pre-designed? [1]

IV

So much for some of the more obvious facts
of the discussion of design *versus* chance, as causal
principles of nature and of life as a whole. We
brought up this discussion, you recall, as a crucial
instance. What does our touchstone indicate as
to the bearing of Darwinian ideas upon philosophy? In the first place, the new logic outlaws,
flanks, dismisses—what you will—one type of
problems and substitutes for it another type.
Philosophy forswears inquiry after absolute origins
and absolute finalities in order to explore specific
values and the specific conditions that generate
them.

Darwin concluded that the impossibility of
assigning the world to chance as a whole and to
design in its parts indicated the insolubility of
the question. Two radically different reasons,

[1] "Life and Letters," Vol. II., pp. 146, 170, 245; Vol. I.,
pp. 283-84. See also the closing portion of his " Variations
of Animals and Plants under Domestication."

however, may be given as to why a problem is insoluble. One reason is that the problem is too high for intelligence; the other is that the question in its very asking makes assumptions that render the question meaningless. The latter alternative is unerringly pointed to in the celebrated case of design *versus* chance. Once admit that the sole verifiable or fruitful object of knowledge is the particular set of changes that generate the object of study together with the consequences that then flow from it, and no intelligible question can be asked about what, by assumption, lies outside. To assert—as is often asserted—that specific values of particular truth, social bonds and forms of beauty, if they can be shown to be generated by concretely knowable conditions, are meaningless and in vain; to assert that they are justified only when they and their particular causes and effects have all at once been gathered up into some inclusive first cause and some exhaustive final goal, is intellectual atavism. Such argumentation is reversion to the logic that explained the extinction of fire by water through the formal essence of aqueousness and the quenching of thirst by water through the final cause of aqueousness. Whether used in the case of the special event or that of life as a whole, such logic only abstracts some aspect of the existing course of events in order to reduplicate it as a petrified eternal principle by which to explain the very changes of which it is the formalization.

When Henry Sidgwick casually remarked in a letter that as he grew older his interest in what or who made the world was altered into interest in what kind of a world it is anyway, his voicing of a common experience of our own day illustrates also the nature of that intellectual transformation effected by the Darwinian logic. Interest shifts from the wholesale essence back of special changes to the question of how special changes serve and defeat concrete purposes; shifts from an intelligence that shaped things once for all to the particular intelligences which things are even now shaping; shifts from an ultimate goal of good to the direct increments of justice and happiness that intelligent administration of existent conditions may beget and that present carelessness or stupidity will destroy or forego.

In the second place, the classic type of logic inevitably set philosophy upon proving that life *must* have certain qualities and values—no matter how experience presents the matter—because of some remote cause and eventual goal. The duty of wholesale justification inevitably accompanies all thinking that makes the meaning of special occurrences depend upon something that once and for all lies behind them. The habit of derogating from present meanings and uses prevents our looking the facts of experience in the face; it prevents serious acknowledgment of the evils they present and serious concern with the goods they promise but do not as yet fulfil. It turns thought to the business of finding a wholesale transcendent remedy for the one and guarantee for the other. One is reminded of the way many moralists and theologians greeted Herbert Spencer's recognition of an unknowable energy from which welled up the phenomenal physical processes without and the conscious operations within. Merely because Spencer labeled his unknowable energy " God," this faded piece of metaphysical goods was greeted as an important and grateful concession to the reality of the spiritual realm. Were it not for the deep hold of the habit of seeking justification for ideal values in the remote and transcendent, surely this reference of them to an unknowable absolute would be despised in comparison with the demonstrations of experience that knowable energies are daily generating about us precious values.

The displacing of this wholesale type of philosophy will doubtless not arrive by sheer logical disproof, but rather by growing recognition of its futility. Were it a thousand times true that opium produces sleep because of its dormitive energy, yet the inducing of sleep in the tired, and the recovery to waking life of the poisoned, would not be thereby one least step forwarded. And were it a thousand times dialectically demonstrated that life as a whole is regulated by a transcendent principle to a final inclusive goal, none the less truth and error, health and disease, good and evil, hope and fear in the concrete, would remain just what and where they now are. To improve our education, to ameliorate our manners, to advance our politics, we must have recourse to specific conditions of generation.

Finally, the new logic introduces responsibility into the intellectual life. To idealize and rationalize the universe at large is after all a confession of inability to master the courses of things that specifically concern us. As long as mankind suffered from this impotency, it naturally shifted a burden of responsibility that it could not carry over to the more competent shoulders of the transcendent cause. But if insight into specific conditions of value and into specific consequences of ideas is possible, philosophy must in time become a method of locating and interpreting the more serious of the conflicts that occur in life, and a method of projecting ways for dealing with them: a method of moral and political diagnosis and prognosis.

The claim to formulate *a priori* the legislative constitution of the universe is by its nature a claim that may lead to elaborate dialectic developments. But it is also one that removes these very conclusions from subjection to experimental test, for, by definition, these results make no differences in the detailed course of events. But a philosophy that humbles its pretensions to the work of projecting hypotheses for the education and conduct of mind, individual and social, is thereby subjected to test by the way in which the ideas it propounds work out in practice. In having modesty forced upon it, philosophy also acquires responsibility.

Doubtless I seem to have violated the implied promise of my earlier remarks and to have turned both prophet and partizan. But in anticipating the direction of the transformations in philosophy to be wrought by the Darwinian genetic and experimental logic, I do not profess to speak for any save those who yield themselves consciously or unconsciously to this logic. No one can fairly deny that at present there are two effects of the Darwinian mode of thinking. On the one hand, there are making many sincere and vital efforts to revise our traditional philosophic conceptions in accordance with its demands. On the other hand, there is as definitely a recrudescence of absolutistic philosophies; an assertion of a type of philosophic knowing distinct from that of the sciences, one which opens to us another kind of reality from that to which the sciences give access; an appeal through experience to something

that essentially goes beyond experience.   This reaction affects popular creeds and religious movements as well as technical philosophies.   The very
conquest of the biological sciences by the new ideas
has led many to proclaim an explicit and rigid
separation of philosophy from science.

Old ideas give way slowly; for they are more
than abstract logical forms and categories.   They
are habits, predispositions, deeply engrained attitudes of aversion and preference.   Moreover, the
conviction persists—though history shows it to be
a hallucination—that all the questions that the
human mind has asked are questions that can be
answered in terms of the alternatives that the questions themselves present.   But in fact intellectual
progress usually occurs through sheer abandonment
of questions together with both of the alternatives
they assume—an abandonment that results from
their decreasing vitality and a change of urgent
interest.   We do not solve them: we get over them.
Old questions are solved by disappearing, evapo-
rating, while new questions corresponding to the
changed attitude of endeavor and preference take
their place.   Doubtless the greatest dissolvent in
contemporary thought of old questions, the greatest precipitant of new methods, new intentions, new
problems, is the one effected by the scientific revolution that found its climax in the " Origin of
Species."

NATURE AND ITS GOOD:
A CONVERSATION [1]

A GROUP of people are scattered near one another, on the sands of an ocean beach; wraps, baskets, etc., testify to a day's outing. Above the hum of the varied conversations are heard the mock sobs of one of the party.

Various voices. What's the matter, Eaton?

Eaton. Matter enough. I was watching a beautiful wave; its lines were perfect; at its crest, the light glinting through its infinitely varied and delicate curves of foam made a picture more ravishing than any dream. And now it has gone; it will never come back. So I weep.

Grimes. That's right, Eaton; give it to them. Of course well-fed and well-read persons—with their possessions of wealth and of knowledge both gained at the expense of others—finally get bored; then they wax sentimental over their boredom and are worried about "Nature" and its relation to life. Not everybody takes it out that way, of course; some take motor cars and champagne for that tired feeling. But the rest—those who aren't

[1] Reprinted from the *Hibbert Journal,* Vol. VII., No. 4, July, 1909.

in that class financially, or who consider themselves too refined for that kind of relief—seek a new sensation in speculating why that brute old world out there will not stand for what you call spiritual and ideal values—for short, your egotisms.

The fact is that the whole discussion is only a symptom of the leisure class disease. If you had to work to the limit and beyond, to keep soul and body together, and, more than that, to keep alive the soul of your family in its body, you would know the difference between your artificial problems and the genuine problem of life. Your philosophic problems about the relation of " the universe to moral and spiritual good " exist only in the sentimentalism that generates them. The genuine question is why social arrangements will not permit the amply sufficient body of natural resources to sustain all men and women in security and decent comfort, with a margin for the cultivation of their human instincts of sociability, love of knowledge and of art.

As I read Plato, philosophy began with some sense of its essentially political basis and mission— a recognition that its problems were those of the organization of a just social order. But it soon got lost in dreams of another world; and even those of you philosophers who pride yourselves on being so advanced that you no longer believe in " another world," are still living and thinking with reference to it.   You may not call it supernatural; but when you talk about a realm of spiritual or ideal values in general, and ask about its relation to Nature in general, you have only changed the labels on the bottles, not the contents in them. For what makes anything transcendental—that is, in common language, supernatural—is simply and only aloofness from practical affairs—which affairs in their ultimate analysis are the business of making a living.

Eaton.   Yes; Grimes has about hit off the point of my little parable—in one of its aspects at least. In matters of daily life you say a man is " off," more or less insane, when he deliberately goes on looking for a certain kind of result from conditions which he has already found to be such that they cannot possibly yield it.   If he keeps on looking, and then goes about mourning because stage money won't buy beefsteaks, or because he cannot keep himself warm by burning the sea-sands here, you dismiss him as a fool or a hysteric.   If you would condescend to reason with him at all, you would tell him to look for the conditions that will yield the results; to occupy himself with some of the countless goods of life for which, by intelligently directed search, adequate means may be found.

Well, before lunch, Moore was reiterating the old tale. " Modern science has completely trans-

formed our conceptions of Nature. It has stripped
the universe bare not only of all the moral values
which it wore alike to antique pagan and to our
medieval ancestors, but also of any regard, any
preference, for such values. They are mere inci-
dents, transitory accidents, in her everlasting redistribution of matter in motion; like the rise and
fall of the wave I lament, or like a single musical
note that a screeching, rumbling railway train
might happen to emit." This is a one-sided view;
but suppose it were all so, what is the moral?
Surely, to change our standpoint, our angle of
vision; to stop looking for results among conditions that we know will not yield them; to turn our
gaze to the goods, the values that exist actually
and indubitably in experience; and consider by
what natural conditions these particular values
may be strengthened and widened.

Insist, if you please, that Nature as a whole
does not stand for good as a whole. Then, in
heaven's name, just because good is both so plural
(so " numerous ") and so partial, bend your energies of intelligence and of effort to selecting the
specific plural and partial natural conditions which
will at least render values that we do have more
secure and more extensive. Any other course is
the way of madness; it is the way of the spoilt
child who cries at the seashore because the waves
do not stand still, and who cries even more franti-

cally in the mountains because the hills do not melt
and flow.

But no.   Moore and his school will not have it
so: we must " go back of the returns."   All this
science, after all, is a mode of knowledge.   Ex-
amine knowledge itself and find it implies a complete all-inclusive intelligence; and then find (by
taking another tack) that intelligence involves
sentiency, feeling, and also will.   Hence your very
physical science, if you will only criticise it, ex-
amine it, shows that its object, mechanical nature,
is itself an included and superseded element in an
all-embracing spiritual and ideal whole.   And there
you are.

Well, I do not now insist that all this is mere
dialectic prestidigitation.   No; accept it; let it go
at its face value.   But what of it?   Is any value
more concretely and securely in life than it was
before?   Does this perfect intelligence enable us
to correct one single mis-step, one paltry error,
here and now?   Does this perfect all-inclusive
goodness serve to heal one disease?   Does it rectify
one trangression?   Does it even give the slightest
inkling of how to go to work at any of these
things?   No; it just tells you: Never mind, for
they are already eternally corrected, eternally
healed in the eternal consciousness which alone is
really Real.   Stop: there is one evil, one pain,
which the doctrine mitigates—the hysteric senti-

mentalism which is troubled because the universe as a whole does not sustain good as a whole. But that is the only thing it alters. The " pathetic fallacy " of Ruskin magnified to the *n*th power is the *motif* of modern idealism.

Moore. Certainly nobody will accuse Eaton of tender-mindedness—except in his logic, which, *as* certainly, is not tough-minded. His excitement, however, convinces me that he has at least an ink-ling that he is begging the question; and like the true pragmatist that he is, is trying to prevent by action (to wit, his flood of speech) his false logic from becoming articulate to him. The ques-tion being whether the values we seem to appre-hend, the purposes we entertain, the goods we pos-sess, are anything more than transitory waves, Eaton meets it by saying: " Oh, of course, they are waves; but don't think about that—just sit down hard on the wave or get another wave to but-tress it with! " No wonder he recommends action instead of thinking! Men have tried this method before, as a counsel of desperation or as cynical pessimism. But it remained for contemporary pragmatism to label the drowning of sorrow in the intoxication of thoughtless action, the highest achievement of philosophic method, and to preach wilful restlessness as a doctrine of hope and illu-mination. Meantime, I prefer to be tender-minded in my attitude toward Reality, and to make that attitude more reasonable by a tough-minded logic.

Eaton. I am willing to be quiet long enough for you to translate your metaphor into logic, and show how I have begged the question.

Moore. It is plain enough. You bid us turn to the cultivation, the nurture, of certain values in human life. But the question is whether these are or are not values. And that is a question of their relation to the Universe—to Reality. If Reality substantiates them, then indeed they are values; if it mocks and flouts them—as it surely does if what mechanical science calls Nature be ultimate and absolute—then they are *not* values. You and your kind are really the sentimentalists, because you are sheer subjectivists. You say: Accept the dream as real; do not question about it; add a little iridescence to its fog and extend it till it obscure even more of Reality than it naturally does, and all is well! I say: Perhaps the dream is no dream but an intimation of the solidest and most ultimate of all realities; and a thorough examination of what the positivist, the materialist, accepts as solid, namely, science, reveals as its own aim, standard, and presupposition that Reality is one all-exhaustive spiritual Being.

Eaton. This is about the way I thought my begging of the question would turn out. You in-

sist upon translating my position into terms of
your own; I am not then surprised to hear that it
would be a begging of the question for *you* to hold
my views. My point is precisely that it is only
as long as you take the position that some Reality
beyond—some metaphysical or transcendental reality—is necessary to substantiate empirical values
that you can even discuss whether the latter are
genuine or illusions. Drop the presupposition that
you read into everything I say, the idea that the
reality of things as they are is dependent upon something beyond and behind, and the facts of the case
just stare you in the eyes: Goods *are*, a multitude
of them—but, unfortunately, evils also *are;* and
all grades, pretty much, of both. Not the contrast and relation of experience *in toto* to something beyond experience drives men to religion and
then to philosophy; but the contrast *within* experience of the better and the worse, and the consequent problem of how to substantiate the former
and reduce the latter. Until you set up the notion of a transcendental reality at large, you cannot even raise the question of whether goods and
evils are, or only seem to be. The trouble and the
joy, the good and the evil, is *that* they are; the
hope is that they may be regulated, guided, increased in one direction and minimized in another.
Instead of neglecting thought, we (I mean the
pragmatists) exalt it, because we say that intelli-

gent discrimination of means and ends is the sole
final resource in this problem of all problems, the
control of the factors of good and ill in life.   We
say, indeed, not merely that that is what intelligence *does*, but rather what it *is*.

Historically, it is quite possible to show how
under certain social conditions this human and
practical problem of the relation of good and intelligence generated the notion of the transcendental good and the pure reason.   As Grimes reminded us, Plato——

Moore.   Yes, and Protagoras—don't forget
him; for unfortunately we know both the origin
and the consequences of your doctrine that being
and seeming are the same.   We know quite well
that pure empiricism leads to the identification
of being and seeming, and that is just why every
deeply moral and religious soul from the time of
Plato and Aristotle to the present has insisted upon
a transcendent reality.

Eaton.   Personally I don't need an absolute to
enable me to distinguish between, say, the good
of kindness and the evil of slander, or the good of
health and the evil of valetudinarianism.   In experience, things bear their own specific characters.
Nor has the absolute idealist as yet answered the
question of *how* the absolute reality enables him
to distinguish between being and seeming in one
single concrete case.   The trouble is that for him

all Being is on the other side of experience, and *all* experience is seeming.

Grimes. I think I heard you mention history. I wish both of you would drop dialectics and go to history. You would find history to be a struggle for existence—for bread, for a roof, for protected and nourished offspring. You would find history a picture of the masses always going under—just missing—in the struggle, because others have captured the control of natural resources, which in themselves, if not as benign as the eighteenth century imagined, are at least abundantly ample for the needs of all. But because of the monopolization of Nature by a few persons, most men and women only stick their heads above the welter just enough to catch a glimpse of better things, then to be shoved down and under. The only problem of the relation of Nature to human good which is real is the economic problem of the exploitation of natural resources in the equal interests of all, instead of in the unequal interests of a class. The problem you two men are discussing has no existence—and never had any—outside of the heads of a few metaphysicians. The latter would never have amounted to anything, would never have had any career at all, had not shrewd monopolists or tyrants (with the skill that characterizes them) have seen that these speculations about reality and a transcendental world could be

distilled into opiates and distributed among the
masses to make them less rebellious. That, if you
would know, Eaton, is the real historic origin of
the ideal world beyond. When you realize that,
you will perceive that the pragmatists are only
half-way over. You will see that practical questions *are* practical, and are not to be solved merely
by having a theory *about* theory different from
the traditional one—which is all your pragmatism
comes to.

Moore. If you mean that your own crass Phi-
listinism is all that pragmatism comes to, I fancy
you are about right. Forget that the only end of
action is to bring about an approximation to the
complete inclusive consciousness; make, as the
pragmatists do, consciousness a means to action,
and one form of external activity is just as good as
another. Art, religion, all the generous reaches
of science which do not show up immediately in
the factory—these things become meaningless, and
all that remains is that hard and dry satisfaction
of economic wants which is Grimes's ideal.

Grimes. An ideal which exists, by the way, only
in your imagination. I know of no more convincing proof of the futile irrelevancy of idealism than
the damning way in which it narrows the content
of actual daily life in the minds of those who up-
hold idealism. I sometimes think I am the only
true idealist. If the conditions of an equitable and

ample physical existence for all were once secured, I, for one, have no fears as to the bloom and harvest of art and science, and all the " higher " things of leisure.   Life is interesting enough for me; give it a show for all.

Arthur.   I find myself in a peculiar position in respect to this discussion.   An analysis of what is involved in this peculiarity may throw some light on the points at issue, for I have to believe that analysis and definition of what exists is the essential matter both in resolution of doubts and in steps at reform.   For brevity, not from conceit, I will put the peculiarity to which I refer in a personal form.   I do not believe for a moment in some different Reality beyond and behind Nature. I do not believe that a manipulation of the logical implications of science can give results which are to be put in the place of those which Science herself yields in her direct application.   I accept Nature as something which is, not seems, and Science as her faithful transcript.   Yet because I believe these things, not in spite of them, I believe in the existence of purpose and of good.   How Eaton can believe that fulfilment and the increasing realization of purpose can exist in human consciousness unless they first exist in the world which is revealed in that consciousness is as much beyond me as how Moore can believe that a manipulation of the method of knowledge can yield considerations of a totally different order from those directly obtained by use of the method. If purpose and fulfilment exist as natural goods, then, and only then, can consciousness itself be a fulfilment of Nature, and be also a natural good. Any other view is inexplicable to sound thinking—save, historically, as a product of modern political individualism and literary romanticism which have combined to produce that idealistic philosophy according to which the mind in knowing the universe creates it.

The view that purpose and realization are profoundly natural, and that consciousness—or, if you will, experience—is itself a culmination and climax of Nature, is not a new view. Formulated by Aristotle, it has always persisted wherever the traditions of sound thinking have not been obscured by romanticism. The modern scientific doctrine of evolution confirms and specifies the metaphysical insight of Aristotle. This doctrine sets forth in detail, and in verified detail, as a genuine characteristic of existence, the tendency toward cumulative results, the definite trend of things toward culmination and achievement. It describes the universe as possessing, in terms of and by right of its own subject-matter (not as an addition of subsequent reflection), differences of value and importance—differences, moreover, that exercise selective influence upon the course of things, that is to say, genuinely determine the events that occur.

It tells us that consciousness itself is such a cumulative and culminating natural event.   Hence it is relevant to the world in which it dwells, and its determinations of value are not arbitrary, not *obiter dicta*, but descriptions of Nature herself.

Recall the words of Spencer which Moore quoted this morning: " There is no pleasure in the consciousness of being an infinitesimal bubble on a globe that is infinitesimal compared with the totality of things.   Those on whom the unpitying rush of changes inflicts sufferings which are often without remedy, find no consolation in the thought that they are at the mercy of blind forces,—which cause indifferently now the destruction of a sun and now the death of an animalcule.   Contemplation of a universe which is without conceivable beginning or end and without intelligible purpose, yields no satisfaction."   I am naïve enough to believe that the only question is whether the object of our " consciousness," of our " thought," of our " contemplation," is or is not as the quotation states it to be. If the statement be correct, pragmatism, like subjectivism (of which I suspect it is only a variation, putting emphasis upon will instead of idea), is an invitation to close our eyes to what is, in order to encourage the delusion that things are other than they are.   But the case is not so desperate.   Speaking dogmatically, the account given of the universe is just—not true.   And the doctrine of evo-

lution of which Spencer professedly made so much
is the evidence.   A universe describable in evolutionary terms is a universe which shows, not indeed
design, but tendency and purpose; which exhibits
achievement, not indeed of a single end, but of a
multiplicity of natural goods at whose apex is consciousness.   No account of the universe in terms
merely of the redistribution of matter in motion is
complete, no matter how true as far as it goes, for
it ignores the cardinal fact that the character of
matter in motion and of its redistribution is such
as cumulatively to achieve ends—to effect the
world of values we know.   Deny this and you deny
evolution; admit it and you admit purpose in the
only objective—that is, the only intelligible—sense
of that term.   I do not say that in addition to the
mechanism there are other ideal causes or factors
which intervene.   I only insist that the whole story
be told, that the character of the mechanism be
noted—namely, that it is such as to produce and
sustain good in a multiplicity of forms.   Mechanism is the mechanism of achieving results.   To ignore this is to refuse to open our eyes to the total
aspects of existence.

Among these multiple natural goods, I repeat, is
consciousness itself.   One of the ends in which Nature genuinely terminates is just awareness of itself—of its processes and ends.   For note the implication as to why consciousness is a natural good:

not because it is cut off and exists in isolation, nor yet because we may, pragmatically, cut off and cultivate certain values which have no existence beyond it; but because it *is* good that things should be known in their own characters.   And this view carries with it a precious result: to know things as they are is to know them as culminating in consciousness; it is to know that the universe genuinely achieves and maintains its own self-manifestation.

A final word as to the bearing of this view upon Grimes's position.   To conceive of human history as a scene of struggle of classes for domination, a struggle caused by love of power or greed for gain, is the very mythology of the emotions.   What we call history is largely non-human, but so far as it is human, it is dominated by intelligence: history is the history of increasing consciousness.   Not that intelligence is actually sovereign in life, but that at least it is sovereign over stupidity, error, and ignorance.   The acknowledgment of things as they are—that is the causal source of every step in progress.   Our present system of industry is not the product of greed or tyrannic lust of power, but of physical science giving the mastery over the mechanism of Nature's energy.   If the existing system is ever displaced, it will be displaced not by good intentions and vague sentiments, but by a more extensive insight into Nature's secrets.

Modern sentimentalism is revolted at the frank

naturalism of Aristotle in saying that some are slaves by nature and others free by nature. But let socialism come to-morrow and somebody—not anybody, but *some*body—will be managing its machinery and somebody else will be managed by the machinery. I do not wonder that my socialistic friends always imagine themselves active in the first capacity—perhaps by way of compensation for doing all of the imagining and none of the executive management at present. But those who are managed, who are controlled, deserve at least a moment's attention. Would you not at once agree that if there is any justice at all in these positions of relative inferiority and superiority, it is because those who are capable by insight deserve to rule, and those who are incapable on account of ignorance, deserve to be ruled? If so, how do you differ, save verbally, from Aristotle?

Or do you think that all that men want in order to *be* men is to have their bellies filled, with assurance of constant plenty and without too much antecedent labor? No; believe me, Grimes, men *are* men, and hence their aspiration is for the divine— even when they know it not; their desire is for the ruling element, for intelligence. Till they achieve that they will still be discontented, rebellious, unruly—and hence ruled—shuffle your social cards as much as you may.

Grimes (after shrugging his shoulders contempt-

uously, finally says): There is one thing I like
about Arthur: he is frank. He comes out with
what you in all your hearts really believe—theory,
supreme and sublime. All is to the good in this
best of all possible worlds, if only some one be
defining and classifying and syllogizing, according to the lines already laid down. Aristotle's God
of pure intelligence (as *he* well knew) was the
glorification of leisure; and Arthur's point of view,
if Arthur but knew it, is as much the intellectual
snobbery of a leisure class economy, as the luxury
and display he condemns are its material snobbery.
There is really nothing more to be said.

Moore. To get back into the game which
Grimes despises. Doesn't Arthur practically say
that the universe is good because it culminates in
intelligence, and that intelligence is good because
it perceives that the universe culminates in—itself?
And, on this theory, are ignorance and error,
and consequent evil, any less genuine achievements of Nature than intelligence and good?
And on what basis does he call by the titles of
achievement and end that which at best is an
infinitesimally fragmentary and transitory episode? I said Eaton begged the question. Arthur
seems to regard it as proof of a superior intelligence (one which realistically takes things as they
are) to beg the question. What is this Nature,
this universe in which evil is as stubborn a fact as

good, in which good is constantly destroyed by the very power that produces it, in which there resides a temporary bird of passage—consciousness doomed to ultimate extinction—what is such a Nature (all that Arthur offers us) save the problem, the contradiction originally in question? A complacent optimism may gloss over its intrinsic self-contradictions, but a more serious mind is forced to go behind and beyond this scene to a permanent good which includes and transcends goods defeated and hopes suborned. Not because idealists have refused to note the facts as they are, but precisely because Nature is, on its face, such a scene as Arthur describes, idealists have always held that it is but Appearance, and have attempted to mount through it to Reality.

Stair. I had not thought to say anything. My attitude is so different from that of any one of you that it seemed unnecessary to inject another varying opinion where already disagreement reigns. But when Arthur was speaking, I felt that perhaps this disagreement exists precisely because the solvent word had not been uttered. For, at bottom, all of you agree with Arthur, and that is the cause of your disagreement with him and one another. You have agreed to make reason, intellect in some sense, the final umpire. But reason, intellect, is the principle of analysis, of division, of discord. When I appeal to feeling as the ultimate organ

of unity, and hence of truth, you smile courteously;
say—or think—mysticism; and the case for you
is dismissed. Words like feeling, sensation, immediate appreciation, self-communication of Being,
I must indeed use when I try to tell the truth I see.
But I well know how inadequate the words are.
And why? Because language is the chosen tool
of intelligence, and hence inevitably bewrayeth the
truth it would convey. But remember that words
are but symbols, and that intelligence must dwell
in the realm of symbols, and you realize a way out.
These words, sensation, feeling, etc., as I utter
them are but invitations to woo you to put yourselves into the one attitude that reveals truth—
an attitude of direct vision.

The beatific vision? Yes, and No. No, if you
mean something rare, extreme, almost abnormal.
Yes, if you mean the commonest and most convincing, the *only* convincing self-impartation of the ultimate good in the scale of goods; the vision of
blessedness in God. For this doctrine is empirical;
mysticism is the heart of all positive empiricism,
of all empiricism which is not more interested in
denying rationalism than in asserting itself. The
mystical experience marks every man's realization
of the supremacy of good, and hence measures the
distance that separates him from pure materialism.
And since the unmitigated materialist is the rarest
of creatures, and the man with faith in an unseen

good the commonest, every man is a mystic—and the most so in his best moments.

What an idle contradiction that Moore and Arthur should try to adduce proofs of the supremacy of ideal values in the universe! The sole possible proof is the proof that actually exists—the direct unhindered realization of those values. For each value brings with it of necessity its own depth of being. Let the pride of intellect and the pride of will cease their clamor, and in the silences Being speaks its own final word, not an argument or external ground of belief, but the self-impartation of itself to the soul. Who are the prophets and teachers of the ages? Those who have been accessible at the greatest depths to these communications.

Grimes. I suppose that poverty—and possibly disease—are specially competent ministers to the spiritual vision? The moral is obvious. Economic changes are purely irrelevant, because purely material and external. Indeed, upon the whole, efforts at reform are undesirable, for they distract attention from the fact that the final thing, the vision of good, is totally disconnected from external circumstance. I do not say, Stair, you personally believe this; but is not such a quietism the logical conclusion of all mysticism?

Stair. This is not so true as to say that in your efforts at reform you are really inspired by the divine vision of justice; and that this mystic vision and not the mere increase of quantity of eatables and drinkables is your animating motive.

Grimes. Well, to my mind this whole affair of mystical values and experiences comes down to a simple straight-away proposition. The submerged masses do not occupy themselves with such questions as those you are discussing. They haven't the time even to consider whether they want to consider them. Nor does the occasional free citizen who even now exists—a sporadic reminder and prophecy of ultimate democracy—bother himself about the relation of the cosmos to value. Why? Not from mystic insight any more than from metaphysical proof; but because he has so many other interests that are worth while. His friends, his vocation and avocations, his books, his music, his club—these things engage him and they reward him. To multiply such men with such interests— that is the genuine problem, I repeat; and it is a problem to be solved only through an economic and material redistribution.

Eaton. Gladly, Stair, do all of us absolve ourselves from the responsibility of having to create the goods that life—call it God or Nature or Chance—provides. But we cannot, if we would, absolve ourselves from responsibility for maintaining and extending these goods when they have happened. To find it very wonderful—as Arthur

does—that intelligence perceives values as they are
is trivial, for it is only an elaborate way of saying
that they have happened.   To invite us, ceasing
struggle and effort, to commune with Being through
the moments of insight and joy that life provides,
is to bid us to self-indulgence—to enjoyment at
the expense of those upon whom the burden of con-
ducting life's affairs falls.   For even the mystics
still need to eat and drink, be clothed and housed,
and somebody must do these unmystic things.   And
to ignore others in the interest of our own perfection is not conducive to genuine unity of Being.

Intelligence is, indeed, as you say, discrimination, distinction.   But why?   Because we have to
act in order to keep secure amid the moving flux
of circumstance, some slight but precious good that
Nature has bestowed; and because, in order to act
successfully, we must act after conscious selection
—after discrimination of means and ends.   Of
course, all goods arrive, as Arthur says, as natural
results, but so do all bads, and all grades of good
and bad.   To label the results that occur culmina-
tions, achievements, and then argue to a quasi-
moral constitution of Nature because she effects
such results, is to employ a logic which applies to
the life-cycle of the germ that, in achieving itself,
kills man with malaria, as well as to the process of
human life that in reaching its fullness cuts short
the germ-fulfilment.   It is putting the cart before

the horse to say that because Nature is so constituted as to produce results of all types of value,
therefore Nature is actuated by regard for differences of value.   Nature, till it produces a being
who strives and who thinks in order that he may
strive more effectively, does not know whether it
cares more for justice or for cruelty, more for the
ravenous wolf-like competition of the struggle for
existence, or for the improvements incidentally introduced through that struggle.   Literally it has
no mind of its own.   Nor would the mere intro-
duction of a consciousness that pictured indifferently the scene out of which consciousness developed, add one iota of reason for attributing eulo-
gistically to Nature regard for value.   But when
the sentient organism, having experienced natural
values, good and bad, begins to select, to prefer,
and to make battle for its preference; and in order
that it may make the most gallant fight possible
picks out and gathers together in perception
and thought what is favorable to its aims and
what hostile, then and there Nature has at last
achieved significant regard for good.   And this is
the same thing as the birth of intelligence.   For
the holding an end in view and the selecting and organizing out of the natural flux, on the basis of
this end, conditions that are means, *is* intelligence.
Not, then, when Nature produces health or efficiency or complexity does Nature exhibit regard

for value, but only when it produces a living organism that has settled preferences and endeavors. The mere happening of complexity, health, adjustment, is all that Nature effects, as rightly called accident as purpose. But when Nature produces an intelligence—ah, then, indeed Nature has achieved something. Not, however, because this intelligence impartially pictures the nature which has produced it, but because in human consciousness Nature becomes genuinely partial. Because in consciousness an end is preferred, is selected for maintenance, and because intelligence pictures not a world just as it is *in toto*, but images forth the conditions and obstacles of the continued maintenance of the selected good. For in an experience where values are demonstrably precarious, an intelligence that is not a principle of emphasis and valuation (an intelligence which defines, describes, and classifies merely for the sake of knowledge,) is a principle of stupidity and catastrophe.

As for Grimes, it is indeed true that problems are solved only where they arise—namely, in action, in the adjustments of behavior. But, for good or for evil, they can be solved there only with method; and ultimately method is intelligence, and intelligence is method. The larger, the more human, the less technical the problem of practice, the more open-eyed and wide-viewing must be the corresponding method. I do not say that all things that have been called philosophy participate in this method; I do say, however, that a catholic and far-sighted theory of the adjustment of the conflicting factors of life *is*—whatever it be called—philosophy.   And unless technical philosophy is to go the way of dogmatic theology, it must loyally identify itself with such a view of its own aim and destiny.

INTELLIGENCE AND MORALS [1]

"EXCEPT the blind forces of nature," said Sir Henry Maine, " nothing moves in this world which is not Greek in its origin." And if we ask why this is so, the response comes that the Greek discovered the business of man to be pursuit of good, and intelligence to be central in this quest. The utmost to be said in praise of Plato and Aristotle is not that they invented excellent moral theories, but that they rose to the opportunity which the spectacle of Greek life afforded. For Athens presented an all but complete microcosm for the study of the interaction of social organization and individual character. A public life of rich diversity in concentrated and intense splendor trained the civic sense. Strife of faction and the rapid oscillations of types of polity provided the occasion for intellectual inquiry and analysis. The careers of dramatic personalities, habits of discussion, ease of legislative change, facilities for personal ambi-

[1] A public lecture delivered at Columbia University in March, 1908, under the title of " Ethics," in a series of lectures on " Science, Philosophy, and Art." Reprinted from a monograph published by the Columbia University Press.

46

tions, distraction by personal rivalries, fixed attention upon the elements of character, and upon consideration of the effect of individual character on social vitality and stability. Happy exemption from ecclesiastic preoccupations, susceptibility to natural harmony, and natural piety conspired with frank and open observation to acknowledgment of the rôle played by natural conditions. Social instability and shock made equally pertinent and obvious the remark that only intelligence can confirm the values that natural conditions generate, and that intelligence is itself nurtured and matured only in a free and stable society.

In Plato the resultant analysis of the mutual implications of the individual, the social and the natural, converged in the ideas that morals and philosophy are one: namely, a love of that wisdom which is the source of secure and social good; that mathematics and the natural sciences focused upon the problem of the perception of the good furnish the materials of moral science; that logic is the method of the pregnant organization of social conditions with respect to good; that politics and psychology are sciences of one and the same human nature, taken first in the large and then in the little. So far that large and expansive vision of Plato.

But projection of a better life must be based upon reflection of the life already lived. The inevitable limitations of the Greek city-state were inevitably wrought into the texture of moral theory.

The business of thought was to furnish a substitute for customs which were then relaxing from the pressure of contact and intercourse without and the friction of strife within. Reason was to take the place of custom as a guide of life; but it was to furnish rules as final, as unalterable as those of custom. In short, the thinkers were fascinated by the afterglow of custom. They took for their own ideal the distillation from custom of its essence —ends and laws which should be rigid and invariable. Thus Morals was set upon the track which it dared not leave for nigh twenty-five hundred years: search for *the* final good, and for *the* single moral force.

Aristotle's assertions that the state exists by nature, and that in the state alone does the individual achieve independence and completeness of life, are indeed pregnant sayings. But as uttered by Aristotle they meant that, in an isolated state, the Greek city-state, set a garlanded island in the waste sea of *barbaroi*, a community indifferent when not hostile to all other social groupings, individuals attain their full end. In a social unity which signified social contraction, contempt, and antagonism, in a social order which despised intercourse and glorified war, is realized the life of excellence!

There is likewise a profound saying of Aristotle's that the individual who otherwise than by accident is not a member of a state is either a brute or a god. But it is generally forgotten that elsewhere Aristotle identified the highest excellence, the chief virtue, with pure thought, and identifying this with the divine, isolated it in lonely grandeur from the life of society. That man, so far as in him lay, should be godlike, meant that he should be non-social, because supra-civic. Plato the idealist had shared the belief that reason is the divine; but he was also a reformer and a radical and he would have those who attained rational insight descend again into the civic cave, and in its obscurity labor patiently for the enlightenment of its blear-eyed inhabitants. Aristotle, the conservative and the definer of what is, gloried in the exaltation of intelligence in man above civic excellence and social need; and thereby isolated the life of truest knowledge from contact with social experience and from responsibility for discrimination of values in the course of life.

Moral theory, however, accepted from social custom more than its cataleptic rigidity, its exclusive area of common good, and its unfructified and irresponsible reason. The city-state was a superficial layer of cultured citizens, cultured through a participation in affairs made possible by relief from economic pursuits, superimposed upon the dense mass of serfs, artizans, and laborers.   For this division, moral philosophy made itself spiritual sponsor, and thus took it up into its own being.   Plato wrestled valiantly with the class problem; but his outcome was the necessity of decisive demarcation, after education, of the masses in whom reason was asleep and appetite much awake, from the few who were fit to rule because alertly wise.   The most generously imaginative soul of all philosophy could not far outrun the institutional practices of his people and his times.   This might have warned his successors of the danger of deserting the sober path of a critical discernment of the better and the worse within contemporary life for the more exciting adventure of a final determination of absolute good and evil.   It might have taught the probability that some brute residuum or unrationalized social habit would be erected into an apotheosis of pure reason.   But the lesson was not learned. Aristotle promptly yielded to the besetting sin of all philosophers, the idealization of the existent: he declared that the class distinctions of superiority and inferiority as between man and woman, master and slave, liberal-minded and base mechanic, exist and are justified by nature—a nature which aims at embodied reason.

What, finally, is this Nature to which the philosophy of society and the individual so bound itself? It is the nature which figures in Greek customs and myth; the nature resplendent and adorned which confronts us in Greek poetry and art: the animism of savage man purged of grossness and generalized by unerring esthetic taste into beauty and system.   The myths had told of the loves and hates, the caprices and desertions of the gods, and behind them all, inevitable Fate.   Philosophy translated these tales into formulæ of the brute fluctuation of rapacious change held in bounds by the final and supreme end: the rational good. The animism of the popular mind died to reappear as cosmology.

Repeatedly in this course we have heard of sciences which began as parts of philosophy and which gradually won their independence.   Another statement of the same history is that both science and philosophy began in subjection to mythological animism.   Both began with acceptance of a nature whose irregularities displayed the meaningless variability of foolish wants held within the limits of order and uniformity by an underlying movement toward a final and stable purpose.   And when the sciences gradually assumed the task of reducing irregular caprice to regular conjunction, philosophy bravely took upon itself the task of substantiating, under the caption of a spiritual view of the universe, the animistic survival.   Doubtless Socrates brought philosophy to earth; but his injunction to man to know himself was incredibly compromised in its execution by the fact that later philosophers submerged man in the world to which philosophy was brought: a world which was the heavy and sunken center of hierarchic heavens located in their purity and refinement as remotely as possible from the gross and muddy vesture of earth.

The various limitations of Greek custom, its hostile indifference to all outside the narrow city-state, its assumption of fixed divisions of wise and blind among men, its inability socially to utilize science, its subordination of human intention to cosmic aim—all of these things were worked into moral theory. Philosophy had no active hand in producing the condition of barbarism in Europe from the fifth to the fifteenth centuries. By an unwitting irony which would have shocked none so much as the lucid moralists of Athens, their philosophic idealization, under captions of Nature and Reason, of the inherent limitations of Athenian society and Greek science, furnished the intellectual tools for defining, standardizing, and justifying all the fundamental clefts and antagonisms of feudalism. When practical conditions are not frozen in men's imagination into crystalline truths, they are naturally fluid. They come and go. But when intelligence fixes fluctuating circumstances into final ideals, petrifaction is likely to occur; and philosophy gratuitously took upon itself the responsibility for justifying the worst defects of barbarian Europe by showing their necessary connection with divine reason.

The division of mankind into the two camps of the redeemed and the condemned had not needed philosophy to produce it. But the Greek cleavage of men into separate kinds on the basis of their position within or without the city-state was used to rationalize this harsh intolerance. The hierarchic organization of feudalism, within church and state, of those possessed of sacred rule and those whose sole excellence was obedience, did not require moral theory to generate or explain it. But it took philosophy to furnish the intellectual tools by which such chance episodes were emblazoned upon the cosmic heavens as a grandiose spiritual achievement. No; it is all too easy to explain bitter intolerance and desire for domination. Stubborn as they are, it was only when Greek moral theory had put underneath them the distinction between the irrational and the rational, between divine truth and good and corrupt and weak human appetite, that intolerance on system and earthly domination for the sake of eternal excellence were philosophically sanctioned. The health and welfare of the body and the securing for all of a sure and a prosperous livelihood were not matters for which medieval conditions fostered care in any case. But moral philosophy was prevailed upon to damn the body on principle, and to relegate to insignificance as merely mundane and temporal the problem of a just industrial order.   Circumstances of the times bore with sufficient hardness upon successful scientific investigation; but philosophy added the conviction that in any case truth is so supernal that it must be supernaturally revealed, and so important that it must be authoritatively imparted and enforced.   Intelligence was diverted from the critical consideration of the natural sources and social consequences of better and worse into the channel of metaphysical subtleties and systems, acceptance of which was made essential to participation in the social order and in rational excellence.   Philosophy bound the once erect form of human endeavor and progress to the chariot wheels of cosmology and theology.

Since the Renaissance, moral philosophy has repeatedly reverted to the Greek ideal of natural excellence realized in social life, under the fostering care of intelligence in action.   The return, however, has taken place under the influence of democratic polity, commercial expansion, and scientific reorganization.   It has been a liberation more than a reversion.   This combined return and emancipation, having transformed our practice of life in the last four centuries, will not be content till it has written itself clear in our theory of that practice.

Whether the consequent revolution in moral philosophy be termed pragmatism or be given the happier title of the applied and experimental habit of mind is of little account. What is of moment is that intelligence has descended from its lonely isolation at the remote edge of things, whence it operated as unmoved mover and ultimate good, to take its seat in the moving affairs of men. Theory may therefore become responsible to the practices that have generated it; the good be connected with nature, but with nature naturally, not metaphysically, conceived, and social life be cherished in behalf of its own immediate possibilities, not on the ground of its remote connections with a cosmic reason and an absolute end.

There is a notion, more familiar than correct, that Greek thought sacrificed the individual to the state. None has ever known better than the Greek that the individual comes to himself and to his own only in association with others. But Greek thought subjected, as we have seen, both state and individual to an external cosmic order; and thereby it inevitably restricted the free use in doubt, inquiry, and experimentation, of the human intelligence. The *anima libera*, the free mind of the sixteenth century, of Galileo and his successors, was the counterpart of the disintegration of cosmology and its animistic teleology. The lecturer on political economy reminded us that his subject began, in the Middle Ages, as a branch of ethics, though, as he hastened to show, it soon got into better association. Well, the same company was once kept by all the sciences, mathematical and physical as well as social. According to all accounts it was the integrity of the number one and the rectitude of the square that attracted the attention of Pythagoras to arithmetic and geometry as promising fields of study. Astronomy was the projected picture book of a cosmic object lesson in morals, Dante's transcript of which is none the less literal because poetic. If physics alone remained outside the moral fold, while noble essences redeemed chemistry, occult forces blessed physiology, and the immaterial soul exalted psychology, physics is the exception that proves the rule: matter was so inherently immoral that no high-minded science would demean itself by contact with it.

If we do not join with many in lamenting the stripping from nature of those idealistic properties in which animism survived, if we do not mourn the secession of the sciences from ethics, it is because the abandonment by intelligence of a fixed and static moral end was the necessary precondition of a free and progressive science of both things and morals; because the emancipation of the sciences from ready made, remote, and abstract values was necessary to make the sciences available for creating and maintaining more and specific values here

and now. The divine comedy of modern medicine
and hygiene is one of the human epics yet to be
written; but when composed it may prove no unworthy companion of the medieval epic of other
worldly beatific visions. The great ideas of the
eighteenth century, that expansive epoch of moral
perception which ranks in illumination and fervor
along with classic Greek thought, the great ideas
of the indefinitely continuous progress of humanity
and of the power and significance of freed intelligence, were borne by a single mother—experimental inquiry.

The growth of industry and commerce is at once
cause and effect of the growth in science. Democ-
ritus and other ancients conceived the mechanical
theory of the universe. The notion was not only
blank and repellent, because it ignored the rich
social material which Plato and Aristotle had organized into their rival idealistic views; but it was
scientifically sterile, a piece of dialectics. Contempt for machines as the accouterments of despised mechanics kept the mechanical conception
aloof from these specific and controllable experiences which alone could fructify it. This conception, then, like the idealistic, was translated into a
speculative cosmology and thrown like a vast net
around the universe at large, as if to keep it from
coming to pieces. It is from respect for the lever,
the pulley, and the screw that modern experimental

and mathematical mechanics derives itself. Motion, traced through the workings of a machine, was followed out into natural events and studied just as motion, not as a poor yet necessary device for realizing final causes. So studied, it was found to be available for new machines and new applications, which in creating new ends also promoted new wants, and thereby stimulated new activities, new discoveries, and new inventions. The recognition that natural energy can be systematically applied, through experimental observation, to the satisfaction and multiplication of concrete wants is doubtless the greatest single discovery ever imported into the life of man—save perhaps the discovery of language. Science, borrowing from industry, repaid the debt with interest, and has made the control of natural forces for the aims of life so inevitable that for the first time man is relieved from overhanging fear, with its wolflike scramble to possess and accumulate, and is freed to consider the more gracious question of securing to all an ample and liberal life. The industrial life had been condemned by Greek exaltation of abstract thought and by Greek contempt for labor, as representing the brute struggle of carnal appetite for its own satiety. The industrial movement, offspring of science, restored it to its central position in morals. When Adam Smith made economic activity the moving spring of man's unremitting effort, from the cradle to the grave, to better his own lot, he recorded this change. And when he made sympathy the central spring in man's conscious moral endeavor, he reported the effect which the increasing intercourse of men, due primarily to commerce, had in breaking down suspicion and jealousy and in liberating man's kindlier impulses.

Democracy, the crucial expression of modern life, is not so much an addition to the scientific and industrial tendencies as it is the perception of their social or spiritual meaning. Democracy is an absurdity where faith in the individual as individual is impossible; and this faith is impossible when intelligence is regarded as a cosmic power, not an adjustment and application of individual tendencies. It is also impossible when appetites and desires are conceived to be the dominant factor in the constitution of most men's characters, and when appetite and desire are conceived to be manifestations of the disorderly and unruly principle of nature. To put the intellectual center of gravity in the objective cosmos, outside of men's own experiments and tests, and then to invite the application of individual intelligence to the determination of society, is to invite chaos. To hold that want is mere negative flux and hence requires external fixation by reason, and then to invite the wants to give free play to themselves in social construction and intercourse, is to call down anarchy. Democracy is estimable only through the changed conception of intelligence, that forms modern science, and of want, that forms modern industry. It is essentially a changed psychology. The substitution, for *a priori* truth and deduction, of fluent doubt and inquiry meant trust in human nature in the concrete; in individual honesty, curiosity, and sympathy. The substitution of moving commerce for fixed custom meant a view of wants as the dynamics of social progress, not as the pathology of private greed. The nineteenth century indeed turned sour on that somewhat complacent optimism in which the eighteenth century rested: the ideas that the intelligent self-love of individuals would conduce to social cohesion, and competition among individuals usher in the kingdom of social welfare. But the conception of a social harmony of interests in which the achievement by each individual of his own freedom should contribute to a like perfecting of the powers of all, through a fraternally organized society, is the permanent contribution of the industrial movement to morals —even though so far it be but the contribution of a problem.

Intellectually speaking, the centuries since the fourteenth are the true middle ages. They mark the transitional period of mental habit, as the so-called medieval period represents the petrifaction, under changed outward conditions, of Greek ideas.

The conscious articulation of genuinely modern tendencies has yet to come, and till it comes the ethic of our own life must remain undescribed. But the system of morals which has come nearest to the reflection of the movements of science, democracy, and commerce, is doubtless the utilitarian. Scientific, after the modern mode, it certainly would be. Newton's influence dyes deep the moral thought of the eighteenth century. The arrangements of the solar system had been described in terms of a homogeneous matter and motion, worked by two opposed and compensating forces: all because a method of analysis, of generalization by analogy, and of mathematical deduction back to new empirical details had been followed. The imagination of the eighteenth century was a Newtonian imagination; and this no less in social than in physical matters. Hume proclaims that morals is about to become an experimental science. Just as, almost in our own day, Mill's interest in a method for social science led him to reformulate the logic of experimental inquiry, so all the great men of the Enlightenment were in search for the organon of morals which should repeat the physical triumphs of Newton. Bentham notes that physics has had its Bacon and Newton; that morals has had its Bacon in Helvétius, but still awaits its Newton; and he leaves us in no doubt that at the moment of writing he was ready, modestly but firmly, to fill the waiting niche with its missing figure.

The industrial movement furnished the concrete imagery for this ethical renovation. The utilitarians borrowed from Adam Smith the notion that through industrial exchange in a free society the individual pursuing his own good is led, under the guidance of the " invisible hand," to promote the general good more effectually than if he had set out to do it. This idea was dressed out in the atomistic psychology which Hartley built out from Locke—and was returned at usurious rates to later economists.

From the great French writers who had sought to justify and promote democratic individualism, ·came the conception that, since it is perverted political institutions which deprave individuals and bring them into hostility, nation against nation, class against class, individual against individual, the great political problem is such a reform of law and legislation, civil and criminal, of administration, and of education as will force the individual to find his own interests in pursuits conducing to the welfare of others.

Tremendously effective as a tool of criticism, operative in abolition and elimination, utilitarianism failed to measure up to the constructive needs of the time. Its theoretical equalization of the good of each with that of every other was practically perverted by its excessive interest in the middle and manufacturing classes. Its speculative defect of an atomistic psychology combined with this narrowness of vision to make light of the constructive work that needs to be done by the state, before all can have, otherwise than in name, an equal chance to count in the common good. Thus the age-long subordination of economics to politics was revenged in the submerging of both politics and ethics in a narrow theory of economic profit; and utilitarianism, in its orthodox descendants, proffered the disjointed pieces of a mechanism, with a monotonous reiteration that looked at aright they form a beautifully harmonious organism.

Prevision, and to some extent experience, of this failure, conjoined with differing social traditions and ambitions, evoked German idealism, the transcendental morals of Kant and his successors. German thought strove to preserve the traditions which bound culture to the past, while revising these traditions to render them capable of meeting novel conditions. It found weapons at hand in the conceptions borrowed by Roman law from Stoic philosophy, and in the conceptions by which Protestant humanism had re-edited scholastic Catholicism. Grotius had made the idea of natural law, natural right and obligation, the central idea of German morals, as thoroughly as Locke had made the individual desire for liberty and happiness the

focus of English and then of French speculation.
Materialized idealism is the happy monstrosity in
which the popular demand for vivid imagery is
most easily reconciled with the equally strong demand for supremacy of moral values; and the complete idealistic materialism of Stoicism has always
given its ideas a practical influence out of all pro-
portion to their theoretical vogue as a system.
To the Protestant, that is the German, humanist,
Natural Law, the bond of harmonious reason in
nature, the spring of social intercourse among
men, the inward light of individual conscience,
united Cicero, St. Paul, and Luther in blessed
union; gave a rational, not superrational basis for
morals, and provided room for social legislation
which at the same time could easily be held back
from too ruthless application to dominant class interests.

Kant saw the mass of empirical and hence irrelevant detail that had found refuge within this liberal and diffusive reason.   He saw that the idea of
reason could be made self-consistent only by stripping it naked of these empirical accretions.   He
then provided, in his critiques, a somewhat cum-
brous moving van for transferring the resultant
pure or naked reason out of nature and the objective world, and for locating it in new quarters,
with a new stock of goods and new customers.   The
new quarters were particular subjects, individuals;

the stock of goods were the forms of perception and the functions of thought by which empirical flux is woven into durable fabrics; the new customers were a society of individuals in which all are ends in themselves. There ought to be an injunction issued that Kant's saying about Hume's awakening of him should not be quoted save in connection with his other saying that Rousseau brought him to himself, in teaching him that the philosopher is of less account than the laborer in the fields unless he contributes to human freedom. But none the less, the new tenant, the universal reason, and the old homestead, the empirical tumultuous individual, could not get on together. Reason became a mere voice which, having nothing in particular to say, said Law, Duty, in general, leaving to the existing social order of the Prussia of Frederick the Great the congenial task of declaring just what was obligatory in the concrete. The marriage of freedom and authority was thus celebrated with the understanding that sentimental primacy went to the former and practical control to the latter.

The effort to force a universal reason that had been used to the broad domains of the cosmos into the cramped confines of individuality conceived as merely "empirical," a highly particularized creature of sense, could have but one result: an explosion. The products of that explosion constitute the Post-Kantian philosophies. It was the work of

Hegel to attempt to fill in the empty reason of Kant with the concrete contents of history. The voice sounded like the voice of Aristotle, Thomas of Aquino, and Spinoza translated into Swabian German; but the hands were as the hands of Montesquieu, Herder, Condorcet, and the rising historical school. The outcome was the assertion that history is reason, and reason is history: the actual is rational, the rational is the actual. It gave the pleasant appearance (which Hegel did not strenuously discourage) of being specifically an idealization of the Prussian nation, and incidentally a systematized apologetic for the universe at large. But in intellectual and practical effect, it lifted the idea of process above that of fixed origins and fixed ends, and presented the social and moral order, as well as the intellectual, as a scene of becoming, and it located reason somewhere within the struggles of life.

Unstable equilibrium, rapid fermentation, and a succession of explosive reports are thus the chief notes of modern ethics. Scepticism and traditionalism, empiricism and rationalism, crude naturalisms and all-embracing idealisms, flourish side by side—all the more flourish, one suspects, because side by side. Spencer exults because natural science reveals that a rapid transit system of evolution is carrying us automatically to the goal of perfect man in perfect society; and his English idealistic contemporary, Green, is so disturbed by the removal from nature of its moral qualities, that he tries to show that this makes no difference, since nature in any case is constituted and known through a spiritual principle which is as permanent as nature is changing.   An Amiel genteelly laments the decadence of the inner life, while his neighbor Nietzsche brandishes in rude ecstasy the banner of brute survival as a happy omen of the final victory of nobility of mind.   The reasonable conclusion from such a scene is that there is taking place a transformation of attitude towards moral theory rather than mere propagation of varieties among theories. The classic theories all agreed in one regard.   They all alike assumed the existence of *the* end, the *summum bonum*, the final goal; and of *the* separate moral force that moves to that goal.   Moralists have disputed as to whether the end is an aggregate of pleasurable state of consciousness, enjoyment of the divine essence, acknowledgment of the law of duty, or conformity to environment.   So they have disputed as to the path by which the final goal is to be reached: fear or benevolence? reverence for pure law or pity for others? self-love or altruism?   But these very controversies implied that there was but the one end and the one means.

The transformation in attitude, to which I referred, is the growing belief that the proper business of intelligence is discrimination of multiple and present goods and of the varied immediate means of their realization; not search for the one remote aim. The progress of biology has accustomed our minds to the notion that intelligence is not an outside power presiding supremely but statically over the desires and efforts of man, but is a method of adjustment of capacities and conditions within specific situations. History, as the lecturer on that subject told us, has discovered itself in the idea of process. The genetic standpoint makes us aware that the systems of the past are neither fraudulent impostures nor absolute revelations; but are the products of political, economic, and scientific conditions whose change carries with it change of theoretical formulations. The recognition that intelligence is properly an organ of adjustment in difficult situations makes us aware that past theories were of value so far as they helped carry to an issue the social perplexities from which they emerged. But the chief impact of the evolutionary method is upon the present. Theory having learned what it cannot do, is made responsible for the better performance of what needs to be done, and what only a broadly equipped intelligence can undertake: study of the conditions out of which come the obstacles and the resources of adequate life, and developing and testing the ideas that, as working hypotheses, may be used to diminish the causes of evil and to buttress and expand the sources of good. This program is indeed vague, but only unfamiliarity with it could lead one to the conclusion that it is less vague than the idea that there is a single moral ideal and a single moral motive force.

From this point of view there is no separate body of moral rules; no separate system of motive powers; no separate subject-matter of moral knowledge, and hence no such thing as an isolated ethical science. If the business of morals is not to speculate upon man's final end and upon an ultimate standard of right, it is to utilize physiology, anthropology, and psychology to discover all that can be discovered of man, his organic powers and propensities. If its business is not to search for the one separate moral motive, it is to converge all the instrumentalities of the social arts, of law, education, economics, and political science upon the construction of intelligent methods of improving the common lot.

If we still wish to make our peace with the past, and to sum up the plural and changing goods of life in a single word, doubtless the term happiness is the one most apt. But we should again exchange free morals for sterile metaphysics, if we imagine that " happiness " is any less unique than the individuals who experience it; any less complex than the constitution of their capacities, or any less variable than the objects upon which their capacities are directed.

To many timid, albeit sincere, souls of an earlier century, the decay of the doctrine that all true and worthful science is knowledge of final causes seemed fraught with danger to science and to morals. The rival conception of a wide open universe, a universe without bounds in time or space, without final limits of origin or destiny, a universe with the lid off, was a menace. We now face in moral science a similar crisis and like opportunity, as well as share in a like dreadful suspense. The abolition of a fixed and final goal and causal force in nature did not, as matter of fact, render rational conviction less important or less attainable. It was accompanied by the provision of a technique of persistent and detailed inquiry in all special fields of fact, a technique which led to the detection of unsuspected forces and the revelation of undreamed of uses. In like fashion we may anticipate that the abolition of *the* final goal and *the* single motive power and *the* separate and infallible faculty in morals, will quicken inquiry into the diversity of specific goods of experience, fix attention upon their conditions, and bring to light values now dim and obscure. The change may relieve men from responsibility for what they cannot do, but it will promote thoughtful consideration of what they may do and the definition of responsibility for what they do amiss because of failure to think straight and carefully. Absolute goods will fall into the background, but the question of making more sure and extensive the share of all men in natural and social goods will be urgent, a problem not to be escaped nor evaded.

Morals, philosophy, returns to its first love; love of the wisdom that is nurse, as nature is mother, of good. But it returns to the Socratic principle equipped with a multitude of special methods of inquiry and testing; with an organized mass of knowledge, and with control of the arrangements by which industry, law, and education may concentrate upon the problem of the participation by all men and women, up to their capacity of absorption, in all attained values. Morals may then well leave to poetry and to art, the task (so unartistically performed by philosophy since Plato) of gathering together and rounding out, into one abiding picture, the separate and special goods of life. It may leave this task with the assurance that the resultant synthesis will not depict any final and all-inclusive good, but will add just one more specific good to the enjoyable excellencies of life.

Humorous irony shines through most of the harsh glances turned towards the idea of an experimental basis and career for morals. Some shiver in the fear that morals will be plunged into anarchic confusion—a view well expressed by a recent writer in the saying that if the *a priori* and transcendental basis of morals be abandoned " we shall have merely the same certainty that now exists in physics and chemistry "! Elsewhere lurks the apprehension that the progress of scientific method will deliver the purposive freedom of man bound hand and foot to the fatal decrees of iron necessity, called natural law. The notion that laws govern and forces rule is an animistic survival. It is a product of reading nature in terms of politics in order to turn around and then read politics in the light of supposed sanctions of nature. This idea passed from medieval theology into the science of Newton, to whom the universe was the dominion of a sovereign whose laws were the laws of nature. From Newton it passed into the deism of the eighteenth century, whence it migrated into the philosophy of the Enlightenment, to make its last stand in Spencer's philosophy of the fixed environment and the static goal.

No, nature is not an unchangeable order, unwinding itself majestically from the reel of law under the control of deified forces. It is an indefinite congeries of changes. Laws are not governmental regulations which limit change, but are convenient formulations of selected portions of change followed through a longer or shorter period of time, and then registered in statistical forms that are amenable to mathematical manipulation.

That this device of shorthand symbolization presages the subjection of man's intelligent effort to fixity of law and environment is interesting as a culture survival, but is not important for moral theory. Savage and child delight in creating bogeys from which, their origin and structure being conveniently concealed, interesting thrills and shudders may be had. Civilized man in the nineteenth century outdid these bugaboos in his image of a fixed universe hung on a cast-iron framework of fixed, necessary, and universal laws. Knowledge of nature does not mean subjection to predestination, but insight into courses of change; an insight which is formulated in " laws," that is, methods of subsequent procedure.

Knowledge of the process and conditions of physical and social change through experimental science and genetic history has one result with a double name: increase of control, and increase of responsibility; increase of power to direct natural change, and increase of responsibility for its equitable direction toward fuller good. Theory located within progressive practice instead of reigning statically supreme over it, means practice itself made responsible to intelligence; to intelligence which relentlessly scrutinizes the consequences of every practice, and which exacts liability by an equally relentless publicity. As long as morals occupies itself with mere ideals, forces and conditions as they

are will be good enough for " practical " men,
since they are then left free to their own devices
in turning these to their own account.   As long as
moralists plume themselves upon possession of the
domain of the categorical imperative with its bare
precepts, men of executive habits will always be at
their elbows to regulate the concrete social conditions through which the form of law gets its actual
filling of specific injunctions.   When freedom is
conceived to be transcendental, the coercive re-
straint of immediate necessity will lay its harsh
hand upon the mass of men.

In the end, men do what they can do.   They
refrain from doing what they cannot do.   They
do what their own specific powers in conjunction
with the limitations and resources of the environment permit.   The effective control of their powers
is not through precepts, but through the regulation of their conditions.   If this regulation is to
be not merely physical or coercive, but moral, it
must consist of the intelligent selection and determination of the environments in which we act;
and in an intelligent exaction of responsibility for
the use of men's powers.   Theorists inquire after
the " motive " to morality, to virtue and the good,
under such circumstances.   What then, one won-
ders, is their conception of the make-up of human
nature and of its relation to virtue and to goodness?   The pessimism that dictates such a ques-

tion, if it be justified, precludes any consideration of morals.

The diversion of intelligence from discrimination of plural and concrete goods, from noting their conditions and obstacles, and from devising methods for holding men responsible for their concrete use of powers and conditions, has done more than brute love of power to establish inequality and injustice among men. It has done more, because it has confirmed with social sanctions the principle of feudal domination. All men require moral sanctions in their conduct: the consent of their kind. Not getting it otherwise, they go insane to feign it. No man ever lived with the exclusive approval of his own conscience. Hence the vacuum left in practical matters by the remote irrelevancy of transcendental morals has to be filled in somehow. It is filled in. It is filled in with class-codes, class-standards, class-approvals —with codes which recommend the practices and habits already current in a given circle, set, calling, profession, trade, industry, club, or gang. These class-codes always lean back upon and support themselves by the professed ideal code. This latter meets them more than half-way. Being in its pretense a theory for regulating practice, it must demonstrate its practicability. It is uneasy in isolation, and travels hastily to meet with compromise and accommodation the actual situation in all its brute

unrationality. Where the pressure is greatest—
in the habitual practice of the political and economic chieftains—there it accommodates the most.

Class-codes of morals are sanctions, under the
caption of ideals, of uncriticised customs; they are
recommendations, under the head of duties, of what
the members of the class are already most given
to doing. If there are to obtain more equable and
comprehensive principles of action, exacting a
more impartial exercise of natural power and resource in the interests of a common good, members
of a class must no longer rest content in responsibility to a class whose traditions constitute its
conscience, but be made responsible to a society
whose conscience is its free and effectively organized intelligence.

In such a conscience alone will the Socratic injunction to man to know himself be fulfilled.

THE EXPERIMENTAL THEORY OF KNOWLEDGE [1]

IT should be possible to discern and describe a knowing as one identifies any object, concern, or event. It must have its own marks; it must offer characteristic features—as much so as a thunder-storm, the constitution of a State, or a leopard. In the search for this affair, we are first of all desirous for something which is for itself, contemporaneously with its occurrence, a cognition, not something called knowledge by another and from without—whether this other be logician, psychologist, or epistemologist. The "knowledge" may turn out false, and hence no knowledge; but this is an after-affair; it may prove to be rich in fruitage of wisdom, but if this outcome be only wisdom after the event, it does not concern us. What we want is just something which takes itself as knowledge, rightly or wrongly.

[1] Reprinted, with considerable change in the arrangement and in the matter of the latter portion, from *Mind*, Vol. XV., N.S., July, 1906.

I

This means a specific case, a sample. Yet instances are proverbially dangerous—so naïvely and graciously may they beg the questions at issue. Our recourse is to an example so simple, so much on its face as to be as innocent as may be of assumptions. This case we shall gradually complicate, mindful at each step to state just what new elements are introduced. Let us suppose a smell, just a floating odor. This odor may be anchored by supposing that it moves to action; it starts changes that end in picking and enjoying a rose. This description is intended to apply to the course of events witnessed and recounted from without. What sort of a course must it be to constitute a knowledge, or to have somewhere within its career that which deserves this title? The smell, *imprimis*, is there; the movements that it excites are there; the final plucking and gratification are experienced. But, let us say, the smell is not the smell *of* the rose; the resulting change of the organism is not a sense of walking and reaching; the delicious finale is not the fulfilment of the movement, and, through that, of the original smell; " is not," in each case meaning is " not experienced as " such. We may take, in short, these experiences in a brutely serial fashion. The smell, S, is replaced (and displaced) by a felt movement, K, this is replaced by the gratification, *G*.   Viewed from without, as we are now regarding it, there is *S-K-G*. But from within, for itself, it is now *S*, now *K*, now *G*, and so on to the end of the chapter. Nowhere is there looking before and after; memory and anticipation are not born.   Such an experience neither is, in whole or in part, a knowledge, nor does it exercise a cognitive function.

Here, however, we may be halted.   If there is anything present in " consciousness " at all, we may be told (at least we constantly are so told) there must be knowledge of it as present—present, at all events, in " consciousness."   There is, so it is argued, knowledge at least of a simple apprehensive type, knowledge of the acquaintance order, knowledge *that*, even though not knowledge *what*. The smell, it is admitted, does not know *about* anything else, nor is anything known *about* the smell (the same thing, perhaps) ; but the smell is known, either by itself, or by the mind, or by some subject, some unwinking, unremitting eye.   No, we must reply ; there is no apprehension without some (however slight) context; no acquaintance which is not either recognition or expectation.   Acquaintance is presence honored with an escort; presence is introduced as familiar, or an associate springs up to greet it.   Acquaintance always implies a little friendliness ; a trace of re-knowing, of

anticipatory welcome or dread of the trait to follow.

This claim cannot be dismissed as trivial. If
valid, it carries with it the distance between being
and knowing: and the recognition of an element of
mediation, that is, of art, in all knowledge. This
disparity, this transcendence, is not something
which holds of *our* knowledge, of finite knowledge,
just marking the gap between our type of consciousness and some other with which we may contrast it after the manner of the agnostic or the
transcendentalist (who hold so much property in
joint ownership!), but exists because knowing is
knowing, that way of bringing things to bear upon
things which we call reflection—a manipulation of
things experienced in the light one of another.

"Feeling," I read in a recent article, "feeling
is immediately acquainted with its own quality,
with its own subjective being." [1]   How and whence
this duplication in the inwards of feeling into feel-

---

[1] I must remind the reader again of a point already suggested. It is the identification of presence in consciousness
with knowledge as such that leads to setting up *a* mind
(*ego,* subject) which has the peculiar property of knowing
(only so often it knows wrong!), or else that leads to
supplying "sensations" with the peculiar property of sur-
veying their own entrails. Given the correct feeling that
knowledge involves relationship, there being, by supposition,
no other *thing* to which the thing in consciousness is related,
it is forthwith related to a soul substance, or to its ghostly
offspring, a "subject," or to "consciousness" itself.

ing the knower and feeling the known? into feeling
as being and feeling as acquaintance? Let us
frankly deny such monsters. Feeling *is* its own
quality; is its own *specific* (whence and why, once
more, *subjective?*) being. If this statement be
dogmatism, it is at least worth insistent declara-
tion, were it only by way of counter-irritant to that
other dogmatism which asserts that being in " consciousness " is always presence for or in knowledge.
So let us repeat once more, that to *be* a smell (or
anything else) is one thing, to be *known* as smell,
another; to be a " feeling " one thing, to be *known*
as a " feeling " another.[1] The first is thinghood;
existence indubitable, direct; in this way all things
are that are in " consciousness " at all.[2] The
second is *reflected* being, things indicating and calling for other things—something offering the possibility of truth and hence of falsity. The first is

[1] Let us further recall that this theory requires either that
things present shall already be psychical things (feelings,
sensations, etc.), in order to be assimilated to the knowing
mind, subject to consciousness; or else translates genuinely
naïve realism into the miracle of a mind that gets outside itself to lay its ghostly hands upon the things of an
external world.

[2] This means that things may be present *as* known, just as
they be present as hard or soft, agreeable or disgusting,
hoped for or dreaded. The mediacy, or the art of intervention, which characterizes knowledge, indicates precisely the
way in which known things as known are immediately
present.

genuine immediacy; the second is (in the instance discussed) a pseudo-immediacy, which in the same breath that it proclaims its immediacy smuggles in another term (and one which is unexperienced both in itself and in its relation) the subject or " consciousness," to which the immediate is related.[1]

But we need not remain with dogmatic assertions. To be acquainted with a thing or with a person has a definite empirical meaning; we have only to call to mind what it is to be genuinely and empirically acquainted, to have done forever with this uncanny presence which, though bare and simple presence, is yet known, and thus is clothed upon and complicated. To be acquainted with a thing is to be assured (from the standpoint of the experience itself) that it is of such and such a character; that it will behave, if given an opportunity, in such and such a way; that the obviously and flagrantly present trait is associated with fellow traits that will show themselves, if the leadings of the present trait are followed out. To be

[1] If Hume had had a tithe of the interest in the *flux* of perceptions and in *habit*—principles of continuity and of organization—which he had in distinct and isolated existences, he might have saved us both from German *Erkenntnisstheorie,* and from that modern miracle play, the psychology of elements of consciousness, that under the ægis of science, does not hesitate to have psychical elements compound and breed, and in their agile intangibility put to shame the performances of their less acrobatic cousins, physical atoms.

acquainted is to anticipate to some extent, on the basis of prior experience. I am, say, barely acquainted with Mr. Smith: then I have no extended body of associated qualities along with those palpably present, but at least some one suggested trait occurs; his nose, his tone of voice, the place where I saw him, his calling in life, an interesting anecdote about him, etc. To be acquainted is to know what a thing is *like* in some particular. If one is acquainted with the smell of a flower it means that the smell is not just smell, but reminds one of some other experienced thing which stands in continuity with the smell. There is thus supplied a condition of control over or purchase upon what is present, the possibility of translating it into terms of some other trait not now sensibly present.

Let us return to our example. Let us suppose that S is not just displaced by K and then by G. Let us suppose it persists; and persists not as an unchanged S alongside K and G, nor yet as fused with them into a new further quale J. For in such events, we have only the type already considered and rejected. For an observer the new quale might be more complex, or fuller of meaning, than the original S, K, or G, but might not be experienced *as* complex. We might thus suppose a composite photograph which should suggest nothing of the complexity of its origin and structure. In this case we should have simply another picture.

But we may also suppose that the blur of the photograph suggests the superimposition of pictures and something of their character. Then we get another, and for our problem, much more fruitful kind of persistence. We will imagine that the final G assumes this form: Gratification-terminating-movement-induced-by-smell. The smell is still present; it has persisted. It is not present in its original form, but is represented with a quality, an office, that of having excited activity and thereby terminating its career in a certain quale of gratification. It is not S, but Σ ; that is S with an increment of meaning due to maintenance and fulfilment through a process. S is no longer just smell, but smell which has excited and thereby secured.

Here we have a cognitive, but not a cognitional thing. In saying that the smell is finally experienced as *meaning* gratification (through intervening handling, seeing, etc.) and meaning it not in a hapless way, but in a fashion which operates to effect what is meant, we retrospectively attribute intellectual force and function to the smell—and this is what is signified by " cognitive." Yet the smell is not cognitional, because it did not knowingly intend to mean this; but is found, after the event, to have meant it. Nor again is the final experience, the Σ or transformed S, a knowledge. Here again the statement may be challenged.

Those who agree with the denial that bare presence of a quale in "consciousness" constitutes acquaintance and simple apprehension, may now turn against us, saying that experience of fulfilment of meaning is just what we mean by knowledge, and this is just what the Σ of our illustration is. The point is fundamental. As the smell at first was presence or being, less than knowing, so the fulfilment is an experience that is more than knowing. Seeing and handling the flower, enjoying the full meaning of the smell as the odor of just this beautiful thing, is not knowledge because it is more than knowledge.

As this may seem dogmatic, let us suppose that the fulfilment, the realization, experience, is a knowledge. Then how shall it be distinguished from and yet classed with other things called knowledge, viz., reflective, discursive cognitions? Such knowledges are what they are precisely because they are not fulfilments, but intentions, aims, schemes, symbols of overt fulfilment. Knowledge, perceptual and conceptual, of a hunting dog is prerequisite in order that I may really hunt with the hounds. The hunting in turn may increase my knowledge of dogs and their ways. But the knowledge of the dog, *qua* knowledge, remains characteristically marked off from the use of that knowledge in the fulfilment experience, the hunt. The hunt is a *realization* of knowledge; it alone, if you please, verifies, validates, knowledge, or supplies tests of truth. The prior knowledge of the dog, was, if you wish, hypothetical, lacking in assurance or categorical certainty. The hunting, the fulfilling, realizing experience alone *gives* knowledge, because it alone completely assures; makes faith good in works.

Now there is and can be no objection to this definition of knowledge, *provided it is consistently adhered to.* One has as much right to identify knowledge with complete assurance, as I have to identify it with anything else. Considerable justification in the common use of language, in common sense, may be found for defining knowledge as complete assurance. But even upon this definition, the fulfilling experience is not, as such, complete assurance, and hence not a knowledge. Assurance, cognitive validation, and guaranteeship, follow from it, but are not coincident with its occurrence. It *gives*, but *is* not, assurance. The concrete construction of a story, the manipulation of a machine, the hunting with the dogs, is not, so far as it *is* fulfilment, a confirmation of meanings previously entertained as cognitional; that is, is not contemporaneously experienced as such. To think of prior schemes, symbols, meanings, as fulfilled in a subsequent experience, is reflectively to present in their relations to one another both the meanings and the experiences in which they are, as a matter of fact, embodied. This reflective attitude cannot be identical with the fulfilment experience itself; it occurs only in retrospect when the worth of the meanings, or cognitive ideas, is critically inspected in the light of their fulfilment; or it occurs as an interruption of the fulfilling experience. The hunter stops his hunting as a fulfilment to reflect that he made a mistake in his idea of his dog, or again, that his dog is everything he thought he was—that his notion of him is confirmed. Or, the man stops the actual construction of his machine and turns back upon his plan in correction or in admiring estimate of its value. *The fulfilling experience is not of itself knowledge*, then, even if we identify knowledge with fulness of assurance or guarantee. Moreover it gives, affords, assurance only in reference to a situation which we have not yet considered.[1]

Before the category of confirmation or refutation can be introduced, there must be something which *means* to mean something and which therefore can be guaranteed or nullified by the issue—and this is precisely what we have not as yet found. We must return to our instance and introduce a further complication. Let us suppose that the smell quale recurs at a later date, and that it recurs neither as the original *S* nor yet as the

---

[1] In other words, the situation as described is not to be confused with the case of hunting on purpose to test an idea regarding the dog.

final Σ, but as an S' which is fated or charged
with the sense of the possibility of a fulfilment like
unto Σ. The S' that recurs is aware of something else which it means, which it intends to effect
through an operation incited by it and without
which its own presence is abortive, and, so to say,
unjustified, senseless. Now we have an experience
which is *cognitional*, not merely cognitive; which
is contemporaneously aware of meaning something
beyond itself, instead of having this meaning ascribed by another at a later period. *The odor
knows the rose; the rose is known by the odor; and
the import of each term is constituted by the relationship in which it stands to the other.* That
is, the import of the smell is the indicating and
demanding relation which it sustains to the enjoyment of the rose as its fulfilling experience; while
this enjoyment is just the content or definition
of what the smell consciously meant, *i.e.*, meant
to mean. Both the thing meaning and the thing
meant are elements in the same situation. Both
are present, but both are not present in the same
way. In fact, one is present as-*not*-present-in-
the-same-way-in-which-the-other-is. It is present
as something to be rendered present in the same
way through the intervention of an operation.
We must not balk at a purely verbal difficulty.
It suggests a verbal inconsistency to speak of a
thing present-as-absent. But all ideal contents,

all aims (that is, things aimed at) are present in just such fashion. Things can be presented as absent, just as they can be presented as hard or soft, black or white, six inches or fifty rods away from the body. The assumption that an ideal content must be either totally absent, or else present *in just the same fashion* as it will be when it is realized, is not only dogmatic, but self-contradictory. The only way in which an ideal content can be experienced at all is to be presented as *not-present-in-the-same-way* in which something else is present, the latter kind of presence affording the standard or type of *satisfactory* presence. When present in the same way it ceases to be an ideal content. Not a contrast of bare existence over against non-existence, or of present conscious-ness over against reality out of present conscious-ness, but of a satisfactory with an unsatisfactory mode of presence makes the difference between the " really " and the " ideally " present.

In terms of our illustration, handling and en-joying the rose are present, but they are not present in the same way that the smell is present. They are present as *going* to be there in the same way, through an operation which the smell stands sponsor for. The situation is inherently an uneasy one—one in which everything hangs upon the performance of the operation indicated; upon the adequacy of movement as a connecting link, or real adjustment of the thing meaning and the thing meant. Generalizing from the instance, we get the following definition: An experience is a knowledge, if in its quale there is an experienced distinction and connection of two elements of the following sort: *one means or intends the presence of the other in the same fashion in which itself is already present, while the other is that which, while not present in the same fashion, must become so present if the meaning or intention of its companion or yoke-fellow is to be fulfilled through the operation it sets up.*

II

We now return briefly to the question of knowledge as acquaintance, and at greater length to that of knowledge as assurance, or as fulfilment which confirms and validates. With the recurrence of the odor as meaning something beyond itself, there is apprehension, knowledge *that*. One may now say I know what a *rose* smells like; or I know what *this* smell is like; I am acquainted with the rose's agreeable odor. In short, on the basis of a present quality, the odor anticipates and forestalls some further trait.

We have also the conditions of knowledge of the confirmation and refutation type. In the working out of the situation just described, in the transformation, self-indicated and self-demanded, of the tensional into a harmonious or satisfactory situation, fulfilment *or* disappointment results. The odor either does or does not fulfil itself in the rose. The smell as intention is borne out by the facts, or is nullified. As has already been pointed out, the subsequent experience of the fulfilment type is not primarily a confirmation or refutation. Its import is too vital, too urgent to be reduced *in itself* just to the value of testing an intention or meaning.[1] But it gets *in reflection* just such verificatory significance. If the smell's intention is unfulfilled, the discrepancy may throw one back, in reflection, upon the original situation. Interesting developments then occur. The smell meant a rose; and yet it did not (so it turns out) mean a rose; it meant another flower, or something, one can't just tell what. Clearly there is *something*

---

[1] Dr. Moore, in an essay in "Contributions to Logical Theory" has brought out clearly, on the basis of a criticism of the theory of meaning and fulfilment advanced in Royce's "World and Individual," the full consequences of this distinction. I quote one sentence (p. 350): "Surely there is a pretty discernible difference between experience as a purposive idea, and the experience which fulfils this purpose. To call them both 'ideas' is at least confusing." The text above simply adds that there is also a discernible and important difference between experiences which, *de facto,* are purposing and fulfilling (that is, are seen to be such *ab extra*), and those which meant to be such, and are found to be what they meant.

else which enters in; something else beyond the odor as it was first experienced determined the validity of its meaning. Here then, perhaps, we have a transcendental, as distinct from an experimental reference? *Only if this something else makes no difference, or no detectable difference, in the smell itself.* If the utmost observation and reflection can find no difference in the smell quales that fail and those that succeed in executing their intentions, then there is an outside controlling and disturbing factor, which, since it is outside of the situation, can never be utilized in knowledge, and hence can never be employed in any concrete testing or verifying. In this case, knowing depends upon an extra-experimental or transcendental factor. But this very transcendental quality makes both confirmation and refutation, correction, criticism, of the pretensions or meanings of things, impossible. For the conceptions of truth and error, we must, upon the transcendental basis, substitute those of accidental success or failure. Sometimes the intention chances upon one, sometimes upon another. Why or how, the gods only know—and they only if to them the extra-experimental factor is not extra-experimental, but makes a concrete difference in the concrete smell. But fortunately the situation is not one to be thus described. The factor that determines the success or failure, does institute a difference in the thing which means the object, and this difference is detectable, once attention, through failure, has been called to the need of its discovery. At the very least, it makes this difference: the smell is infected with an element of uncertainty of meaning—and this as a part of the thing experienced, not for an observer. This additional *awareness* at least brings about an additional *wariness*. Meaning is more critical, and operation more cautious.

But we need not stop here. Attention may be fully directed to the subject of smells. Smells may become the object of knowledge. They may take, *pro tempore*,[1] the place which the rose formerly occupied. One may, that is, observe the cases in which odors mean other things than just roses, may voluntarily produce new cases for the sake of further inspection, and thus account for the cases where meanings had been falsified in the issue; discriminate more carefully the peculiarities of those meanings which the event verified, and thus safeguard and bulwark to some extent the employing of similar meanings in the future. Superficially, it may then seem as if odors were treated after the fashion of Locke's simple ideas,

[1] The association of science and philosophy with leisure, with a certain economic surplus, is not accidental. It is practically worth while to postpone practice; to substitute theorizing, to develop a new and fascinating mode of practice. But it is the excess achievement of practice which makes this postponement and substitution possible.

or Hume's "distinct ideas which are separate
existences." Smells apparently assume an independent, isolated status during this period of investigation. "Sensations," as the laboratory psychologist and the analytic psychologist generally
studies them, are examples of just such detached
things. But egregious error results if we forget
that this seeming isolation and detachment is the
outcome of a deliberate scientific device—that it is
simply a part of the scientific technique of an inquiry directed upon securing *tested* conclusions.
Just and only because odors (or any group of
qualities) are parts of a connected world are
they signs of things beyond themselves; and only
because they are signs is it profitable and necessary
to study them *as if* they were complete, self-en-
closed entities.

In the reflective determination of things with
reference to their specifically meaning other things,
experiences of fulfilment, disappointment, and going astray inevitably play an important and recurrent *rôle*. They also are realistic facts, related in
realistic ways to the things that intend to mean
other things and to the things intended. When
these fulfilments and refusals *are reflected upon* in
the determinate relations in which they stand to
their relevant meanings, they obtain a quality which
is quite lacking to them in their immediate occurrence as just fulfilments or disappointments; viz.,

the property of affording assurance and correction —of confirming and refuting.   Truth and falsity are not properties of any experience or thing, in and of itself or in its first intention ; *but of things where the problem of assurance consciously enters in.   Truth and falsity present themselves as significant facts only in situations in which specific meanings and their already experienced fulfilments and non-fulfilments are intentionally compared and contrasted with reference to the question of the worth, as to reliability of meaning, of the given meaning or class of meanings.*   Like knowledge itself, truth is an experienced relation of things, and it has no meaning outside of such relation,[1] any more than such adjectives as comfortable applied to a lodging, correct applied to speech, persuasive applied to an orator, etc., have worth apart from the *specific* things to which they are applied.   It would be a great gain for logic and epistemology, if we were always to translate the noun " truth " back into the adjective " true," and this back into the adverb " truly " ;   at least, if we were to do so until we have familiarized ourselves thoroughly

[1] It is the failure to grasp the coupling of truth of meaning with a *specific* promise, undertaking, or intention expressed by a thing which underlies, so far as I can see, the criticisms passed upon the experimental or pragmatic view of the truth.   It is the same failure which is responsible for the wholly *at large* view of truth which characterizes the absolutists.

with the fact that "truth" is an abstract noun, summarizing a quality presented by specific affairs in their own specific contents.

III

I have attempted, in the foregoing pages, a description of the function of knowledge in its own terms and on its merits—a description which in intention is realistic, if by realistic we are content to mean naturalistic, a description undertaken on the basis of what Mr. Santayana has well called "following the lead of the subject-matter." Unfortunately at the present time all such undertakings contend with a serious extraneous obstacle. Accomplishing the undertaking has difficulties enough of its own to reckon with; and first attempts are sure to be imperfect, if not radically wrong. But at present the attempts are not, for the most part, even listened to on their own account, they are not examined and criticised as naturalistic attempts. *They are compared with undertakings of a wholly different nature, with an epistemological theory of knowledge, and the assumptions of this extraneous theory are taken as a ready-made standard by which to test their validity.* Literally of course, "epistemology" means only theory of knowledge; the term *might* therefore have been employed simply as a synonym for a descriptive logic; for a theory that takes knowledge as it finds it and attempts to give the same kind of an account of it that would be given of any other natural function or occurrence. But the mere mention of what *might* have been only accentuates what is. The things that pass for epistemology all assume that knowledge is not a natural function or event, but a mystery.

Epistemology starts from the assumption that certain conditions lie back of knowledge. The mystery would be great enough if knowledge were constituted by non-natural conditions back of knowledge, but the mystery is increased by the fact that the conditions are defined so as to be incompatible with knowledge. Hence the primary problem of epistemology is: How is knowledge *überhaupt*, knowledge at large, *possible?* Because of the incompatibility between the concrete occurrence and function of knowledge and the conditions back of it to which it must conform, a second problem arises: How is knowledge in general, knowledge *überhaupt, valid?* Hence the complete divorce in contemporary thought between epistemology as theory of knowledge and logic as an account of the specific ways in which particular beliefs that are better than other alternative beliefs regarding the same matters are formed; and also the complete divorce between a naturalistic, a biological and social psychology, setting forth how the function of knowledge is evolved out of other natural activities, and epistemology as an account of how knowledge is possible anyhow.

It is out of the question to set forth in this place in detail the contrast between transcendental epistemology and an experimental theory of knowledge. It may assist the understanding of the latter, however, if I point out, baldly and briefly, how, *out of the distinctively empirical situation*, there arise those assumptions which make knowledge a mystery, and hence a topic for a peculiar branch of philosophizing.

As just pointed out, epistemology makes the possibility of knowledge a problem, because it assumes back of knowledge conditions incompatible with the obvious traits of knowledge as it empirically exists. These assumptions are that the organ or instrument of knowledge is not a natural object, but some ready-made state of mind or consciousness, something purely " subjective," a peculiar kind of existence which lives, moves, and has its being in a realm different from things to be known; and that the ultimate goal and content of knowledge is a fixed, ready-made thing which has no organic connections with the origin, purpose, and growth of the attempt to know it, some kind of *Ding-an-sich* or absolute, extra-empirical " Reality."

(1) It is not difficult to see at what point in

the development of natural knowledge, or the signifying of one thing by another, there arises the
notion of the knowing medium as something radically different in the order of existence from the
thing to be known.   It arises subsequent to the repeated experience of non-fulfilment, of frustration
and disappointment.   The odor did not after all
mean the rose; it meant something quite different;
and yet its indicative function was exercised so
forcibly that we could not help—or at least *did*
not help—believing in the existence of the rose.
This is a familiar and typical kind of experience,
one which very early leads to the recognition that
" things are not what they seem."   There are
two contrasted methods of dealing with this recognition: one is the method indicated above (p. 93).
We go more thoroughly, patiently, and carefully
into the facts of the case.   We employ all sorts
of methods, invented for the purpose, of examining the things that are signs and the things that
are signified, and we experimentally produce various situations, in order that we may tell *what* smells
mean roses *when* roses are meant, what it is about
the smell and the rose that led us into error; and
that we may be able to discriminate those cases in
which a suspended conclusion is all that circumstances admit.   We simply do the best we can to
regulate our system of signs so that they become as
instructive as possible, utilizing for this purpose

(as indicated above) all possible experiences of success and of failure, and deliberately instituting cases which will throw light on the specific empirical causes of success and failure.

Now it so happens that when the facts of error were consciously generalized and formulated, namely in Greek thought, such a technique of specific inquiry and rectification did not exist—in fact, it hardly could come into existence until *after* error had been seized upon as constituting a fundamental anomaly. Hence the method just outlined of dealing with the situation was impossible. We can imagine disconsolate ghosts willing to postpone any professed solution of the difficulty till subsequent generations have thrown more light on the question itself; we can hardly imagine passionate human beings exercising such reserve. At all events, Greek thought provided what seemed a satisfactory way out: there are two orders of existence, one permanent and complete, the noumenal region, to which alone the characteristic of Being is properly applicable, the other transitory, phenomenal, sensible, a region of non-Being, or at least of mere Coming-to-be, a region in which Being is hopelessly mixed with non-Being, with the unreal. The former alone is the domain of knowledge, of truth; the latter is the territory of opinion, confusion, and error. In short, the contrast *within* experience of the cases in which things suc-

cessfully and unsuccessfully maintained and executed the meanings of other things was erected into
a wholesale difference of status in the intrinsic
characters of the things involved in the two types
of cases.

With the beginnings of modern thought, the
region of the " unreal," the source of opinion and
error, was located exclusively in the individual.
The object was *all* real and *all* satisfactory, but
the " subject " could approach the object only
through his own subjective states, his " sensations " and " ideas." The Greek conception of
two orders of existence was retained, but instead
of the two orders characterizing the " universe "
itself, one *was* the universe, the other was the
individual mind trying to know that universe.
This scheme would obviously easily account for
error and hallucination; but how could *knowledge*,
truth, ever come about such a basis? The Greek
problem of the possibility of error became
the modern problem of the possibility of knowledge.

Putting the matter in terms that are independent of history, experiences of failure, disappointment, non-fulfilment of the function of meaning and contention may lead the individual to the
path of science—to more careful and extensive
investigation of the things themselves, with a view
to detecting specific sources of error, and guard-

ing against them, and regulating, so far as possible, the conditions under which objects are bearers of meanings beyond themselves. But impatient of such slow and tentative methods (which insure not infallibility but increased probability of valid conclusions), by reason of disappointment a person may turn epistemologist. He may then take the discrepancy, the failure of the smell to execute its own intended meaning, as a wholesale, rather than as a specific fact: as evidence of a contrast in general between things meaning and things meant, instead of as evidence of the need of a more cautious and thorough inspection of odors and execution of operations indicated by them. One may then say: Woe is me; smells are only *my* smells, subjective states existing in an order of being made out of consciousness, while roses exist in another order made out of a radically different sort of stuff; or, odors are made out of "finite" consciousness as their stuff, while the real things, the objects which fulfil them, are made out of an "infinite" consciousness as their material. Hence some purely metaphysical tie has to be called in to bring them into connection with each other. And yet this tie does not concern knowledge; it does not make the meaning of one odor any more correct than that of another, nor enable us to discriminate relative degrees of correctness. As a principle of control, this transcendental connection is related to all alike, and hence condemns and justifies all alike.[1]

It is interesting to note that the transcendentalist almost invariably first falls into the psychological fallacy; and then having himself taken the psychologist's attitude (the attitude which is interested in meanings as themselves self-inclosed " ideas ") accuses the empiricist whom he criticises of having confused mere psychological existence with logical validity. That is, he begins by supposing that the smell of our illustration (and all the cognitional objects for which this is used as a

---

[1] The belief in the *metaphysical* transcendence of the object of knowledge seems to have its real origin in an *empirical* transcendence of a very specific and describable sort. The thing meaning is one thing; the thing meant is another thing, and is (as already pointed out) a thing presented as not given in the same way as is the thing which means. It is something *to be* so given. No amount of careful and thorough inspection of the indicating and signifying things can remove or annihilate this gap. The *probability* of correct meaning may be increased in varying degrees— and this is what we mean by control. But final certitude can never be reached except experimentally—except by performing the operations indicated and discovering whether or no the intended meaning is fulfilled *in propria persona*. In this experimental sense, truth or the object of any given meaning is always beyond or outside of the cognitional thing that means it. Error as well as truth is a necessary function of knowing. But the non-empirical account of this transcendent (or beyond) relationship puts *all* the error in one place (*our* knowledge), and *all* the truth in another (absolute consciousness or else a thing-in-itself).

symbol) is a purely mental or psychical state, so that the question of logical reference or intention is the problem of how the merely mental can " know " the extra-mental. But from a strictly empirical point of view, the smell which knows is no more merely mental than is the rose known. We may, if we please, say that the smell when involving conscious meaning or intention is " mental," but this term " mental " does not denote some separate type of existence—existence as a state of consciousness. It denotes only the fact that the smell, a real and non-psychical object, now exercises an intellectual *function*. This new property involves, as James has pointed out, an *additive* relation—a new property possessed by a non-mental object, when that object, occurring in a new context, assumes a further office and use.[1] To be " in the mind " means to be in a situation in which the function of intending is directly concerned.[2] Will not some one who believes that the knowing experience is *ab origine* a strictly " mental " thing, explain how, as matter of fact, it does get a specific, extra-mental reference, capable of being tested, confirmed, or re-

[1] Compare his essay, " Does Consciousness Exist? " in the *Journal of Philosophy, Psychology, and Scientific Methods,* Vol. I., p. 480.

[2] Compare the essay on the " Problem of Consciousness," by Professor Woodbridge, in the Garman Memorial Volume, entitled " Studies in Philosophy and Psychology."

futed? Or, if he believes that viewing it as merely mental expresses only the form it takes for psychological analysis, will he not explain why he so persistently attributes the inherently "mental" characterization of it to the empiricist whom he criticises? An object *becomes* meaning when used empirically in a certain way; and, under certain circumstances, the exact character and worth of this meaning *becomes* an object of solicitude. But the transcendental epistemologist with his purely psychical "meanings" and his purely extra-empirical "truths" assumes a *Deus ex Machina* whose mechanism is preserved a secret. And as if to add to the arbitrary character of his assumption, he has to admit that the transcendental *a priori* faculty by which mental states get objective reference does not in the least help us to discriminate, *in the concrete*, between an objective reference that is false and one that is valid.

(2) The counterpart assumption to that of pure aboriginal "mental states" is, of course, that of an Absolute Reality, fixed and complete in itself, of which our "mental states" are bare transitory hints, their true meaning and their transcendent goal being the Truth *in rerum natura*. If the organ and medium of knowing is a self-inclosed order of existence different in kind from the Object to be known, then that Object must stand out there in complete aloofness from the concrete purpose

and procedure of knowing it.   But if we go back to
the knowing as a natural occurrence, capable of
description, we find that just as a smell does not
mean Rose in general (or anything else at large),
but means a *specific* group of qualities whose experience is intended and anticipated, so the function of knowing is always expressed in connections
between a given experience and a specific possible
wanted experience.   The " rose " that is meant in a
particular situation *is* the rose of that situation.
When this experience is consummated, it is achieved
as the fulfilment of the conditions in which just
that intention was entertained—not as the fulfilment of a faculty of knowledge or a meaning in
general.   Subsequent meanings and subsequent fulfilments may increase, may enrich the consummat-
ing experience; the object or content of the rose
as known may be other and fuller next time and
so on.   But we have no right to set up " a rose "
at large or in general as the object of the knowing
odor; the object of a knowledge is always strictly
correlative to that particular thing which means it.
It is not something which can be put in a wholesale
way over against that which cognitively refers to
it, as when the epistemologist puts the " real " rose
(object) over against a merely phenomenal or empirical rose which *this* smell happens to mean.   As
the meaning gets more complex, fuller, more finely
discriminated, the object which realizes or fulfils

the meaning grows similarly in quality. But we cannot set up a rose, an object of fullest, complete, and exhaustive content as that which is really meant by any and every odor of a rose, whether it consciously meant to mean it or not. The test of the cognitional rectitude of the odor lies in the *specific* object which it sets out to secure. This is the meaning of the statement that the import of *each* term is found in its relationship to the other. It applies to object meant as well as to the meaning. Fulfilment, completion are always relative terms. *Hence the criterion of the truth or falsity of the meaning, of the adequacy, of the cognitional thing lies within the relationships of the situation and not without.* The thing that means another by means of an intervening operation either succeeds or fails in accomplishing the operation indicated, while this operation either gives or fails to give the object meant. Hence the truth or falsity of the original cognitional object.

IV

From this excursion, I return in conclusion to a brief general characterization of those situations in which we are aware that things mean other things and are so critically aware of it that, in order to increase the probability of fulfilment and to decrease the chance of frustration, all possible pains are taken to regulate the meanings that attach to things. These situations define that type of knowing which we call *scientific*. There are things that claim to mean other experiences; in which the trait of meaning other objects is not discovered *ab extra*, and after the event, but is part of the thing itself. This trait of the thing is as realistic, as specific, as any other of its traits. It is, therefore, as open to inspection and determination as to its nature, as is any other trait. Moreover, since it is upon this trait that assurance (as distinct from accident) of fulfilment depends, an especial interest, an absorbing interest, attaches to its determination. Hence the scientific type of knowledge and its growing domination over other sorts.

We *employ* meanings in all intentional constructions of experience—in all anticipations, whether artistic, utilitarian or technological, social or moral. The success of the anticipation is found to depend upon the character of the meaning. Hence the stress upon a right determination of these meanings. Since they are the instruments upon which fulfilment depends *so far as that is controlled* or other than accidental, they become themselves objects of surpassing interest. For all persons at some times, and for one class of persons (scientists) at almost all times, the determination of the meanings employed in the control of fulfilments (of acting upon meanings) is central.

The experimental or pragmatic theory of knowledge explains the dominating importance of science; it does not depreciate it or explain it away.

Possibly pragmatic writers are to blame for the tendency of their critics to assume that the practice they have in mind is utilitarian in some narrow sense, referring to some preconceived and inferior use—though I cannot recall any evidence for this admission. But what the pragmatic theory has in mind is precisely the fact that all the affairs of life which need regulation—*all values of all types* —depend upon utilizations of meanings. Action is not to be limited to anything less than the carrying out of ideas, than the execution, whether strenuous or easeful, of meanings. Hence the surpassing importance which comes to attach to the careful, impartial construction of the meanings, and to their constant survey and resurvey with reference to their value as evidenced by experiences of fulfilment and deviation.

That truth denotes *truths*, that is, specific verifications, combinations of meanings and outcomes reflectively viewed, is, one may say, the central point of the experimental theory. Truth, in general or in the abstract, is a just name for an experienced relation among the things of experience: that sort of relation in which intents are retrospectively viewed from the standpoint of the fulfilment which they secure through their own natural operation or incitement. Thus the experimental theory explains directly and simply the absolutistic tendency to translate concrete true things into the general relationship, Truth, and then to hypostatize this abstraction into identity with real being, Truth *per se* and *in se*, of which all transitory things and events—that is, all experienced realities —are only shadowy futile approximations. This type of relationship is central for man's will, for man's conscious endeavor. To select, to conserve, to extend, to propagate those meanings which the course of events has generated, to note their peculiarities, to be in advance on the alert for them, to search for them anxiously, to substitute them for meanings that eat up our energy in vain, defines the aim of rational effort and the goal of legitimate ambition. The absolutistic theory is the transfer of this moral or voluntary law of selective action into a quasi-physical (that is, metaphysical) law of indiscriminate being. Identify metaphysical being with *significant excellent* being—that is, with those relationships of things which, in our moments of deepest insight and largest survey, we would continue and reproduce—and the experimentalist, rather than the absolutist, is he who has a right to proclaim the supremacy of Truth, and the superiority of the life devoted to Truth for its own sake over that of " mere " activity. But to read back into an order of things which exists without the participation of our reflection and aim, the quality which defines the purpose of our thought and endeavor is at one and the same stroke to mythologize reality and to deprive the life of thoughtful endeavor of its ground for being.

THE INTELLECTUALIST CRITERION
FOR TRUTH [1]

I

AMONG the influences that have worked in contemporary philosophy towards disintegration of intellectualism of the epistemological type, and towards the substitution of a philosophy of experience, the work of Mr. Bradley must be seriously counted. One has, for example, only to compare his metaphysics with the two fundamental contentions of T. H. Green, namely, that reality is a single, eternal, and all-inclusive system of relations, and that this system of relations is one in kind with that process of relating which constitutes our thinking, to be instantly aware of a changed atmosphere. Much of Bradley's writings is a sustained and deliberate polemic against intellectualism of the Neo-Kantian type. When, however, we find conjoined to this criticism an

[1] Reprinted, with many changes, from an article in *Mind*, Vol. XVI., N.S., July 1907. Although the changes have been made to render the article less technical, it still remains, I fear, too technical to be intelligible to those not familiar with recent discussions of logical theory.

equally sustained contention that the philosophic conception of reality must be based on an exclusively intellectual criterion, a criterion belonging to and confined to theory, we have a situation that is thought-provoking. The situation grows in interest when it is remembered that there is a general and growing tendency among those who appeal in philosophy to a strictly intellectualistic *method* of defining " reality," to insist that the reality reached by this method has a super-intellectual *content:* that intellectual, affectional, and volitional features are all joined and fused in " ultimate " reality. The curious character of the situation is that Reality is an " absolute experience " of which the intellectual is simply one partial and transmuted moment. Yet this reality is attained unto, in philosophic method, by exclusive emphasis upon the intellectual aspect of present experience and by systematic exclusion of exactly the emotional, volitional features which with respect to content are insisted upon! Under such circumstances the cynically-minded are moved to wonder whether this tremendous insistence upon one factor in present experience at the expense of others, is not because this is the only way to maintain the notion of " Absolute Experience," and to prevent it from collapsing into ordinary every-day experience. This paradox is not peculiar to Mr. Bradley. Looking at the Neo-Kantian movement in the broad in its modern form, one might almost say that its prominent feature is its insistence upon reaching a "Reality" that includes extra-intellectual factors and phases, traits that are ideal in a moral and emotional sense, by an exclusive recognition of the function of knowledge in its isolation.

Such being the case, an examination of Mr. Bradley's method and criterion may have far-reaching implications. First, let us set before ourselves the general points of Mr. Bradley's indictment of intellectualism.[1] Knowledge or judgment works by means of thought; it is predication of idea (meaning) of existence as its subject. Its final aim is to effect a complete union or harmony of existence and meaning. But it is fore-doomed to failure, for in realizing its end it must employ means which contradict its own purpose. This inherent incapacity lurks in judgment with respect to subject, predicate, and copula. The predicate or meaning necessary to complete the reality presented in the subject can be referred to the latter and united with it only by being itself alienated from existence. It heals the wounds or deficiencies of its own subject (and in the end all deficiencies are to the modern idealist discrepancies) only on condition of inflicting another wound,—only by sundering meaning from a prior union with exist-

[1] I follow chiefly Chapter XV. of "Appearance and Reality"—the chapter on "Thought and Reality."

ence in some other phase. This latter existence,
therefore, is always left out in the cold. It is as
if we wanted to get all the cloth in the world into
one garment and our only way of accomplishing
this were to tear off a portion from one piece of
goods in order to patch it on to another.

The subject of the judgment, moreover, as well
as the predicate, stands in the way of judgment
fulfilling its own task. It has " sensuous infini-
tude " and it has " immediacy," but these two
traits contradict each other. The details of the
subject always go beyond itself, being indefinitely
related to something beyond. " In its given content it has relations which do not terminate within
that content " (*ibid.*, p. 176), while in its immediacy it presents an undivided union of existence
and meaning. No subject can be mere existence
any more than it can be mere meaning. It is always existent or embodied meaning. As such it
claims individuality or the character of a single
subsistent whole. But this indispensable claim is
inconsistent with its ragged-edged character, its
indefinite external reference, which is indispensable
to it as subject that it may require and receive
further meaning from predication.

With respect to the copula the following quotation from the " Principles " of Logic (p. 10)
may serve: " Judgment proper is the *act* which
refers the ideal content (recognized as such) to the

reality beyond the act." In other words, judgment as act (and it is the act which is expressed in the copula) must always fall outside of the content of knowledge as such; yet since this act certainly falls within reality, it would have to be recognized and stated by any knowledge pretending to competency with respect to reality as a whole. These considerations, stated in this way, are highly technical and presuppose a knowledge not merely of Mr. Bradley's own logic, but also of the logical analysis of knowledge initiated by Kant and carried on by Herbart, Lotze, and others. Their main import may, however, be stated in comparatively non-technical form. Human experience is full of discrepancies. Were experience purely a matter of brute existence (such as we sometimes imagine the animals' experience to be) it would be totally lacking in meaning and there would be no problems, no thinking, no occasion for thinking, and hence no philosophy. On the other hand, if experience were a complete, tight-jointed union of existence and meaning, there would be no dissatisfaction, no problems, no cause for efforts to patch up defects and contradictions. Existences, things, would embody all the meanings that they suggest; while abstract meanings, values that are *merely* ideal, that are projected or thought of but not fulfilled, would be totally unheard of. But our experience stands in marked contrast to both these types of experience. It is neither an affair of meaningless existence nor of existence self-luminous with fulfilled meaning. All things that we experience have *some* meaning, but that meaning is always so partially embodied in things that we cannot rest in them. They point beyond themselves; they indicate meanings which they do not fulfil; they suggest values which they fail to embody, and when we go to other things for the fruition of what is denied, we either find the same situation of division over again, or we find even more positive disappointment and frustration—we find contrary meanings set up. Now all thinking grows out of this discrepancy between existence and the meaning which it partially embodies and partially refuses, which it suggests but declines to express. Yet thinking, the mode of bringing existence and meaning into harmony with each other, always works by selection, by abstraction; it sets up and projects meanings which are ideal only, footless, in the air, matters of thought only, not of sentiency or immediate existence. It emphasizes the ideal of a completed union of existence and meaning, but is helpless to effect it. And this helplessness (according to Mr. Bradley) is not due to external pressure but to the very structure of thought itself.

From every point of view knowledge operates under conditions, (and these not externally imposed but inherent in its own nature as judgment,) that render it incapable of realizing its aim of complete union of existence and meaning. Granted the argument, and it is difficult to imagine a more serious indictment against the pretensions of philosophy to reach " Reality " *via* the exclusive path of knowledge.

The presence of contradiction is Mr. Bradley's criterion for " appearance," just as its absence is his criterion for " reality." It thus goes without saying that knowledge and truth which we can attain are matters of appearance. Contradiction between existence and meaning is its last word. This is not merely a logical deduction from Mr. Bradley's position, but is expressly stated by him. " Thus the truth belongs to existence, but it does not as such exist. . . . Truth shows a dissection but never an actual life " (" Appearance and Reality," p. 167). Again, " every truth is appearance since in it we have divorce of quality from being " (*ibid.*, p. 187). " Even absolute truth seems in the end to turn out erroneous. . . . Internal discrepancy belongs irremovably to truth's proper character. . . . Truth is one aspect of experience and is therefore made imperfect and limited by what it fails to include " (*ibid.*, pp. 544-545). Nothing could be more explicit as to the inherently contradictory character of truth, both as an ideal and as an accom-

plished fact; nothing more positive as to the unreality or appearance-character of truth. We
cannot, on Mr. Bradley's method, stop here. Not
only is knowledge—working as it does through
thought which is always partial, selective, abstrac-
tive—doomed to failure in accomplishing its task,
but the existence of the contradiction between the
suggestion of meanings by existence and this realization in existence is itself due to thought.

Speaking of thought he says: " The relational
form is a compromise on which thought stands and
which it develops." And all the particular anti-
nomies which he discusses are interpreted as having
their basis in the category of relation (*ibid.*,
p. 180). In his section on Appearance he goes
through various aspects and distinctions of the
world, such as primary and secondary qualities,
substance and its properties, relation and qualitative elements, space and time, motion and change,
causation, etc., pointing out irreconcilable discrepancies in them. He does not, in a *generalized* way,
expressly refer them to any common source or root.
But it seems a fair inference that the relational
character of thought is at the bottom of the whole
trouble: so that we have in the cases mentioned
precisely the same situation *in concreto* which
is set forth *in abstracto* in the discussion of
thought. The contradictions brought up are in
every case resolved into the fundamental discrep-

ancy supposed to exist between relations and elements related. In each case there is the ideal of a final unity in which relations and elements as such disappear, while in every case the nature of relation is such as to prevent the desired consummation. In at least one place, it is expressly declared that it is the knowledge function which is responsible for the degradation of reality to appearance. "We do not suggest that the thing always itself is an appearance. We mean its character is such *that it becomes one as soon as we judge it*. And this character we have seen throughout our work, is ideality. Appearance consists in the looseness of content from existence. . . . And we have found that everywhere throughout the world such ideality prevails" (*ibid.*, p. 486, italics not in the original). It is not then strictly true that the divorce of meaning and existence instigates thought; rather thought is the unruly member that creates the divorce and then engages in the task (in which it is self-condemned to failure) of trying to establish the unity which it has gratuitously destroyed. Thinking, self-consciousness, is disease of the naïve unity of thoughtless experience.

On the one hand there is a systematic discrediting of the ultimate claims of the knowledge function, and this not from external physiological or psychological reasons such as are sometimes alleged against its capacity, but on the basis of its own interior logic. But on the other hand, a strictly logical criterion is deliberately adopted and employed as the fundamental and final criterion for the philosophic conception of reality. Long familiarity has not dulled my astonishment at finding exactly the same set of considerations which in the earlier portion of the book are employed to condemn things as experienced by us to the region of Appearance, employed in the latter portion of the book to afford a triumphant demonstration of the existence and character of Absolute Reality. The argument I take up first on its formal side, and then with reference to material considerations.[1]

The positive conception of Reality is reached by the conception that " ultimate reality must be such that it does not contradict itself ; here is an absolute criterion. And it is proved absolute by the fact that either in endeavoring to deny it or even in attempting to doubt it, we tacitly assume its validity " (*ibid.*, pp. 136-137). That is to say, when one sets out to think one must avoid self-contradiction ; this avoidance, or, put positively, the attainment of consistency, harmony, is the basic law of all thinking. Since in thinking we set out to attain reality, it follows that reality itself must be self-consistent, and that its self-consistency

---

[1] The crux of the argument is contained in Chapters XIII. and XIV., on the " General Nature of Reality."

determines the law of thought.   Or, as Mr. Bradley again puts the matter, " In order to think at
all you must subject yourself to the standard, a
standard which implies an absolute knowledge of
reality; and while you doubt this, you accept it,
and obey, while you rebel" (*ibid.*, p. 153).
The absolute knowledge referred to is, of course,
the knowledge of the thoroughly self-consistent,
non-contradictory character of reality.   Every
reader of Mr. Bradley's book knows how he goes
on from this point to supply positive content to
reality; to give an outline sketch of the characters
it must possess and the way in which it must possess
them in order to maintain its thoroughly self-
consistent character.   It is, however, only the
strictly formal aspect of the matter that I am
here concerned with.

On this side we reach, I think, the heart of the
matter by asking, in reference to the first quotation: Absolute *for what?*   Surely absolute for the
process under consideration, that is absolute for
thought.   But the significance of this absolute for
thought is, one may say, " absolutely " (since we
are here confessedly in the realm just of thought)
determined by the nature of thought itself.   Now
this nature has been already referred by considerations " belonging irremovably to truth's proper
character," to the world of appearance and of internal discrepancy.   Yes, one may say (speaking

formally), the criterion of thought is absolute—that is to say absolute or final for thought; but how can one imagine that this in any way alters the essential nature and value of thought? If knowledge works by thought, and thought institutes appearance over against reality, any further fact about thought—such as a statement of its criterion —falls wholly within the limits of this situation. It is comical to suppose that a *special* trait of thought can be employed to alter the fundamental and essential nature of thought. The criterion of thought must be infected by the nature of thought, instead of being a redeeming angel which at a critical juncture transforms the fragile creature, thought, into an ambassador with power plenipotentiary to the court of the Absolute.

There really seems to be ground for supposing that the whole argument turns on an ambiguity in the use of the word " absolute." Keeping strictly within the limits of the argument, it means nothing more than that thinking has a certain principle, a law of its own; that it has an appropriate mode of procedure which must not be violated. It means, in short, whatever is finally controlling for the thought-function. But Mr. Bradley immediately takes the word to mean absolute in the sense of describing a reality which by its very nature is totally contradistinguished from appearance—that is to say, from the realm of thought.

Upon the ambiguity of a word, the systematic indictment of intellectualism becomes the cornerstone of a systematically intellectualistic method of conceiving reality!

Mr. Bradley has himself recognized the seeming contradiction between his indictment of thought and his use of the criterion of thought as the exclusive path to a philosophic notion of the real. In dealing with it, he (to my mind) comes within an ace of stating a truer doctrine, and also exhibits even more clearly the weakness of his own position. He goes so far as to put the following words into the mouth of an objector, and to accept their general import: "All axioms, as a matter of fact, are practical . . . for none of them in the end can amount to more than the impulse to behave in a certain way. And they cannot express more than this impulse, together with the impossibility of satisfaction unless it is complied with" (p. 151). After accepting this (p. 152) he goes on to say: "Take for example the law of avoiding contradiction. When two elements will not remain quietly together, but collide and struggle, we cannot rest satisfied with that state. Our impulse is to alter it and, on the theoretical side, to bring the content to such shape that the variety remains peaceably in one. And this inability to rest otherwise and this tendency to alter in a certain way and direction is, *when reflected*

upon and made explicit, our axiom and our intellectual standard " (p. 152; italics mine).

The retort is obvious: if *the* intellectual criterion, the principle of non-contradiction on which
his whole Absolute Reality rests, is itself a practical principle, then surely the ultimate criterion
for regulating intellectual undertakings is practical.   To this obvious answer Mr. Bradley makes
reply as follows: " You may call the intellect, if
you like, a mere tendency to a movement, but you
must remember that it is a movement of a *very
special kind.* . . . Thinking is the attempt
to satisfy a *special* impulse, and the attempt implies an assumption about reality. . . . But
why, it may be objected, is this assumption better
than what holds for practice?   Why is the theoretical to be superior to the practical end?   I have
never said that this is so, only *here,* that is, in *metaphysics,* I must be allowed to reply, we are acting
theoretically. . . .   The *theoretical standard
within theory must surely be absolute* " (p. 153.
The italics again are mine; compare with the quotation this, from p. 485: " Our attitude, however,
in metaphysics must be theoretical."   So, also, p.
154, " Since metaphysics is mere theory and since
theory from its nature must be made by the intellect, it is here the intellect alone which is to be
satisfied ").

Grant that intellect is a special movement or

mode of practice; grant that we are not merely acting (are we ever *merely* acting?) but are "specially occupied and therefore subject to special conditions," and the problem remains *what* special kind of activity is thinking? what is its experienced differentia from other kinds? what is its commerce with them?   When the problem is *what* special kind of an activity is thinking and of *what* nature is the consistency which is its criterion, somehow we do not get forward by being told that thinking *is* a special mode of practice and that its criterion *is* consistency.   The unquestioned presupposition of Mr. Bradley is that thinking is such a wholly separate activity (the " intellect *alone* " which has to be satisfied), that to give it autonomy is to say that it, and its criterion, have nothing to do with other activities; that it is " independent " as to criterion, in a way which excludes interdependence in function and outcome.   Unless the term "special " be interpreted to mean *isolated*, to say that thinking is a *special* mode of activity no more nullifies the proposition that it arises in a practical contest and operates for practical ends, than to say that blacksmithing is a *special* activity, negates its being one connected mode of industrial activity.

His underlying presupposition of the separate character of thought comes out in the passage last quoted.   " Our impulse," he says, " is to alter the conflicting situation and, *on the theoretical side,* to bring its contents into peaceable unity." If one substitutes for the word " on " the word " through," one gets a conception of theory and of thinking that does justice to the autonomy of the operation and yet so connects it with other activities as to give it a serious business, real purpose, and concrete responsibility and hence testibility. From this point of view the theoretical activity is simply the form that certain practical activities take after colliding, as the most effective and fruitful way of securing their own harmonization. The collision is not theoretical; the issue in " peaceable unity " is not theoretical. But theory names the type of activity by which the transformation from war to peace is most amply and securely effected.[1]

Admit, however, the force of Mr. Bradley's contention on its own terms and see how futile is

[1] The same point comes out in Mr. Bradley's treatment of the way in which the practical demand for the good or satisfaction is to be taken account of in a philosophical conception of the nature of reality. He admits that it comes in; but holds that it enters not directly, but because if left outside it indirectly introduces a feature of " discontent " on the intellectual side (see p. 155). This, as an argument for the supremacy of the isolated theoretical standard, loses all its force if we cease to conceive of intellect as from the start an independent function, and realize that intellectual discontent *is* the practical conflict becoming deliberately aware of itself as the most effective means of its own rectification.

the result.   It is quite true, as Mr. Bradley says (p. 153), that if a man sits down to play the metaphysical game, he must abide by the rules of thinking; but if thinking be already, with respect to reality, an idle and futile game, simply abiding by the rules does not give additional value to its stakes.   Grant the premises as to the character of thought, and the assertion of the final character of the theoretical standard within metaphysics—since metaphysics is a form of theory—is a warning against metaphysics.   If the intellect involves self-contradiction, it is either impossible that it should be satisfied, or else self-contradiction *is* its satisfaction.

II

Let us, however, turn from Mr. Bradley's formal proof that the criterion of philosophic truth must be exclusively a canon of formal thought.   Let us ignore the contradiction involved in first making the work of thought to be the producing of appearance and then making the law of this thought the law of an Absolute Reality.   What about the intellectualist criterion?   The intellectualism of Mr. Bradley's philosophy is represented in the statement that it is " the theoretical standard which guarantees that reality is a self-consistent system " (p. 148).   But how can the fact that the criterion of thinking is consistency be employed to determine the nature of the consistency of its object? Consistency in one sense, consistency of reasoning with itself, we know; but what is the nature of the consistency of reality which this consistency necessitates? Thinking without doubt must be logical; but does it follow from this that the reality about which one thinks, and about which one must think consistently if one is to think to any purpose, must itself be already logical? The pivot of the argument is, of course, the old ontological argument, stripped of all theological irrelevancies and reduced to its fighting weight as a metaphysical proposition. Those who question this basic principle of intellectualism will, of course, question it here. They will urge that, instead of the consistency of " reality " resting on the basis of consistency in the reasoning process the latter derives its meaning from the material consistency at which it aims. They will say that the definition of the nature of the consistency which is the end of thinking and which prescribes its technique is to be reached from inquiry into such questions as these: What sort of an activity in the concrete is thinking? what are the specific conditions which it has to fulfil? what is its use; its relevancy; its purport in present concrete experiences? The more it is insisted that the theoretical standard—consistency—is final within theory, the more germane and the more urgent is the question: What then in the concrete *is* theory? and of what nature *is* the material consistency which is the test of its formal consistency? [1]

Take the instance of a man who wishes to deny the criterion of self-consistency in thinking. Is he refuted by pointing to the " fact " that eternal reality is eternally self-consistent? Would not his obvious answer to such a mode of refutation be: " What of it? What is the relevancy of that proposition to my procedure in thinking here and now? Doubtless absolute reality may be a great number of things, possibly very sublime and precious things; but what I am concerned with is a particular job of thinking, and until you show me the intermediate terms which link that job to the asserted self-consistent character of absolute reality, I fail to see what difference this doubtless

---

[1] This suggests that many of the stock arguments against pragmatism fail to take its contention seriously enough. They proceed from the assumption that it is an account of truth which leaves untouched current notions of the nature of intelligence. But the essential point of pragmatism is that it bases its changed account of truth on a changed conception of the nature of intelligence, both as to its objective and its method. Now this different account of intelligence may be wrong, but controversy which leaves standing the conventionally current theories about thought and merely discusses " truth " will not go far. Since truth is the adequate fulfilment of the function of intelligence, the question turns on the nature of the latter.

wholly amiable trait of reality has to make in what I am here and now concerned with. You might as well quote any other irrelevant fact, such as the height of the Empress of China." We take another tack in dealing with the man in question. We call his attention to his specific aim in the situation with reference to which he is thinking, and point out the conditions that have to be observed if that aim is to fulfil itself. We show that if he does not observe the conditions imposed by his aim his thinking will go on so wildly as to defeat itself. It is to consistency of means with the end of the concrete activity that we appeal. "Try thinking," we tell such a man, "experiment with it, taking pains sometimes to have your reasonings consistent with one another, and at other times deliberately introducing inconsistencies; then see what you get in the two cases and how the result reached is related to your purpose in thinking." We point out that since that purpose is to reach a settled conclusion, that purpose will be defeated unless the steps of reasoning are kept consistent with one another. We do not appeal from the mere consistency of the reasoning process—the intellectual aspect of the matter—to an absolute self-consistent reality; but we appeal from the material character of the end to be reached to the type of the formal procedure necessary to accomplish it.

With all our heart, then, the standard of think-

ing is absolute (that is final) within thinking.
But what is thinking? The standard of blacksmithing must be absolute within blacksmithing,
but what is blacksmithing? No prejudice prevents acknowledging that blacksmithing is one
practical activity existing as a distinct and relevant member of a like system of activities: that it
is because men use horses to transport persons and
goods that horses need to be shod. The ultimate
criterion of blacksmithing is producing a good
shoe, but the nature of a good shoe is fixed,
not by blacksmithing, but by the activities in
which horses are used. The end is ultimate (absolute) for the operation, but this very finality is
evidence that the operation is not absolute and
self-inclosed, but is related and responsible. Why
must the fact that the end of thinking is ultimate
for thought stand on any different footing?

Let us then, by way of experiment, follow this
suggestion. Let us assume that among real objects
in their values and significances, real oppositions
and incompatibilities exist; that these conflicts are
both troublesome in themselves, and the source of
all manner of further difficulties—so much so that
they may be suspected of being the source of all
man's woe, of all encroachment upon and destruction of value, of good. Suppose that thinking
is, not accidentally but essentially, a way, and the
only way that proves adequate, of dealing with

these predicaments—that being " in a hole," in difficulty, is the fundamental " predicament " of intelligence. Suppose when effort is made in a brute way to remove these oppositions and to secure an arrangement of things which means satisfaction, fulfilment, happiness, that the method of brute attack, of trying directly to force warrings into peace fails; suppose then an effort to effect the transformation by an indirect method—by inquiry into the disordered state of affairs and by framing views, conceptions, of what the situation would be like were it reduced to harmonious order. Finally, suppose that upon this basis a plan of action is worked out, and that this plan, when carried into overt effect, succeeds infinitely better than the brute method of attack in bringing about the desired consummation. Suppose again this indirection of activity is precisely what we mean by thinking. Would it not hold that harmony is the end and the test of thinking? that observations are pertinent and ideas correct just in so far as, overtly acted upon, they succeed in removing the undesirable, the inconsistent.

But, it is said, the very process of thinking makes a certain assumption regarding the nature of reality, viz., that reality is self-consistent. This statement puts the end for the beginning. The assumption is not that " reality " *is* self-consistent, but that by thinking it may, for some special purpose, or as respects some concrete problem, attain greater consistency. Why should the assumption regarding "reality" be other than that specific realities with which thought is concerned are *capable of receiving* harmonization? To say that thought must assume, in order to go on, that reality already possesses harmony is to say that thought must begin by contradicting its own direct data, and by assuming that its concrete aim is vain and illusory. Why put upon thought the onus of introducing discrepancies into reality in order just to give itself exercise in the gymnastic of removing them? The assumption that concrete thinking makes about "reality" is that things just as they exist may acquire *through activity, guided by thinking,* a certain character which it is excellent for them to possess; and may acquire it more liberally and effectively than by other methods. One might as well say that the blacksmith could not think to any effect concerning iron, without a Platonic archetypal horseshoe, laid up in the heavens. His thinking also makes an assumption about present, given reality, viz., that this piece of iron, through the exercise of intelligently directed activity, may be shaped into a satisfactory horseshoe. The assumption is practical: the assumption that a specific thing may take on in a specific way a specific needed value. The test, moreover, of this assumption is practical; it consists in acting upon it to see if it will do what it pretends it can do, namely, guide activities to the required result. The assumption about reality is not something in addition to the idea, which an idea already in existence makes; some assumption about the possibility of a change in the state of things as experienced *is* the idea—and its test or criterion is whether this possible change can be effected when the idea is acted upon in good faith.

In any case, how much simpler the case becomes when we stick by the empirical facts. According to them there is no wholesale discrepancy of existence and meaning; there is simply a " loosening " of the two when objects do not fulfil our plans and meet our desires; or when we project inventions and cannot find immediately the means for their realization. The " collisions " are neither physical, metaphysical, nor logical; they are moral and practical. They exist between an aim and the means of its execution. Consequently the object of thinking is not to effect some wholesale and " Absolute " reconciliation of meaning and existence, but to make a specific adjustment of things to our purposes and of our purposes to things at just the crucial point of the crisis. Making the utmost concessions to Mr. Bradley's account of the discrepancy of meaning and existence in our experience, to his statement of the relation of this to the function of judgment (as involving namely an explicit *statement* at once of the actual sundering and the ideal union) and to his account of consistency as the goal and standard, there is still not a detail of the account that is not met amply and with infinitely more empirical warrant by the conception that the " collision " in which thinking starts and the " consistency " in which it terminates are practical and human.

III

This brings us explicitly to the question of truth, " truth " being confessedly the end and standard of thinking.   I confess to being much at a loss to realize just what the intellectualists conceive to be the relation of truth to ideas on one side and to " reality " on the other.   My difficulty occurs, I think, because they describe so little in analytical detail; in writing of truth they seem rather to be under a strong emotional influence— as if they were victims of an uncritical pragma- tism—which leaves much of their thought to be guessed at.   The implication of their discussions assigns three distinct values to the term " truth." On the one hand, truth is something which char- acterizes ideas, theories, hypotheses, beliefs, judg- ments, propositions, assertions, etc.,—anything whatsoever involving *intellectual* statement.   From this standpoint a criterion of truth means the test of the worth of the intellectual intent, import, or claim of any intellectual statement as intellectual. This is an intelligible sense of the term truth.   In the second place, it seems to be assumed that a certain kind of reality is already, apart from ideas or meanings, Truth, and that *this* Truth is the criterion of that lower and more unworthy kind of truth that may be possessed or aimed at by ideas.   But we do not stop here.   The conception that *all* truth must have a criterion haunts the intellectualist, so that the reality, which, as contrasted with ideas, is taken to be The Truth (and the criterion of *their* truth) is treated as if it itself had to have support and warrant from some other Reality, lying back of it, which is *its* criterion. This, then, gives the third type of truth, *The Absolute Truth*.   (Just why this process should not go on indefinitely is not clear, but the necessity of infinite regress may be emotionally prevented by always referring to this last type of truth as Absolute).   Now this scheme may be " true," but it is not self-explanatory or even easily apprehensible.   In just what sense, truth is (1) that to which ideas as ideas lay claim and yet is (2) Reality which as reality is the criterion of truth of ideas, and yet again is (3) a Reality which completely annuls and transcends all reference to ideas, is not in the least clear to me: nor, till better informed, shall I believe it to be clear to any one.

In his more strictly logical discussions, Mr. Bradley sets out from the notion that truth refers to intellectual statements and positions as such. But the Truth soon becomes a sort of transcendent essence on its own account. The identification of reality and truth on page 146 may be a mere casual phrase, but the distinction drawn between validity and absolute truth (p. 362), and the discussion of Degrees of Truth and Reality, involve assumptions of an identity of truth and reality. Truth in this sense turns out to be the criterion for the truth, the truth, that is, of ideas. But, again (p. 545), a distinction is made between "Finite Truth," that is, a view of reality which would completely satisfy intelligence as such, and "Absolute Truth," which is obtained only by *passing beyond intelligence*—only when intelligence as such is absorbed in some Absolute in which it loses its distinctive character.

It would advance the state of discussion, I am sure, if there were more explicit statements regarding the relations of "true idea," "truth," "the criterion of truth" and "reality," to one another. A more explicit exposition also of the view that is held concerning the relation of verification and truth could hardly fail to be of value. Not infrequently the intellectualist admits that the process of verification is experimental, consisting in setting on foot various activities that express the intent of the idea and confirm or refute it according to the changes effected. This seems to mean that truth is simply the tested or verified belief as such. But then a curious reservation is introduced; the experimental process *finds*, it is said, that an idea is true, while the error of the pragmatist is to take the process by which truth is *found* as one by which it is made. The claim of "making truth" is treated as blasphemy against the very notion of truth: such are the consequences of venturing to translate the Latin "verification" into the English "making true."

If we face the bogie thus called up, it will be found that the horror is largely sentimental. Suppose we stick to the notion that truth is a character which belongs to a meaning so far as tested through action that carries it to successful completion. In this case, to make an idea true is to modify and transform it until it reaches this successful outcome: until it initiates a mode of response which in its issue realizes its claim to be the method of harmonizing the discrepancies of a given situation. The meaning is remade by constantly acting upon it, and by introducing into its content such characters as are indicated by any resulting failures to secure harmony. From this point of view, verification and truth are two names for the same thing. We call it " verification " when we regard it as process; when the development of the idea is strung out and exposed to view in all that makes it true. We call it " truth " when we take it as product, as process telescoped and condensed.

Suppose the idea to be an invention, say of the telephone. In this case, is not the verification of the idea and the construction of the device which carries out its intent one and the same? In this case, does the truth of the idea mean anything else than that the issue proves the idea can be carried into effect? There are certain intellectualists who are not of the absolutist type; who do not believe that all of men's aims, designs, projects, that have to do with action, whether industrial, social, or moral in scope, have been from all eternity registered as already accomplished in reality. How do such persons dispose of this problem of the truth of practical ideas?

Is not the truth of *such* ideas an affair of *making* them true by constructing, through appropriate behavior, a condition that satisfies the requirements of the case? If, in this case, truth means the effective capacity of the idea " to make good," what is there in the logic of the case to forbid the application of analogous considerations to any idea?

I hear a noise in the street. It suggests as its meaning a street-car. To test this idea I go to the window and through listening and looking intently—the listening and the looking being modes of behavior—organize into a single situation elements of existence and meaning which were previously disconnected. In this way an idea is made true; that which was a proposal or hypothesis is no longer merely a propounding or a guess. If I had not reacted in a way appropriate to the idea it would have remained a mere idea; at most a candidate for truth that, unless acted upon upon the spot, would always have remained a theory. Now in such a case—where the end to be accomplished is the discovery of a certain order of facts —would the intellectualist claim that apart from the forming and entertaining of some interpretation, the category of truth has either existence or meaning? Will he claim that without an original practical uneasiness introducing a practical aim of inquiry there must have been, whether or no, an idea? Must the world for some purely intellectual reason be intellectually reduplicated? Could not that occurrence which I now identify as a noisy street-car have retained, so far as pure intelligence is concerned, its unidentified status of being mere physical alteration in a vast unidentified complex of matter-in-motion? Was there any *intellectual* necessity that compelled the event to arouse just this judgment, that it meant a street-car? Was there any physical or metaphysical necessity?

Was there any necessity save a need of characterizing it for some purpose of our own? And why should we be mealy-mouthed about calling this need practical? If the necessity which led to the formation and development of an intellectual judgment was purely objective (whether physical or metaphysical) why should not the thing have also to be characterized in countless millions of other ways; for example, as to its distance from some crater in the moon, or its effect upon the circulation of my blood, or upon my irascible neighbor's temper, or bearing upon the Monroe Doctrine? In short, do not intellectual positions and statements mean new and significant events in the treatment of things?

It is perhaps dangerous to attempt to follow the inner workings of the processes by which truth is first identified with some superior type of Reality, and then this Truth is taken as the criterion of the truth of ideas; while all the time it is held that truth is something already possessed by ideas as purely intellectual. But there seems to be some ground for believing that this identification is due to a twofold confusion, one having to do with ideas, and the other with things. As to the first point: After an idea is made true, we naturally say, in retrospect, " it *was* true all the time." Now this truism is quite innocuous as a truism, being just a restatement of the fact that the idea has, as matter of fact, worked successfully. But it may be regarded not as a truism but as furnishing some additional knowledge; as if it were, indeed, the dawning of a revelation regarding truth.   Then it is said that the idea worked or was verified because it was already inherently, just as idea, the truth; the pragmatist, so it is said, making the error of supposing that it is true because it works.   If one remembers that what the experimentalist means is that the effective working of an idea and its truth are one and the same thing—this working being neither the cause nor the evidence of truth but its nature—it is hard to see the point of this statement.   A man under peculiarly precarious circumstances has been rescued from drowning.   A by-stander remarks that now he is a saved man. "Yes," replies some one, "but he was a saved man all the time, and the process of rescuing, while it gives evidence of that fact, does not constitute it." Now even such a statement as pure tautology, as characterizing the entire process in terms of its issue, is objectionable only in the fact that, like all tautology, it seems to say something but does not.   But if it be regarded as revealing the earlier condition of affairs, apart from the active process by which it was carried to a happy conclusion, such a statement would be monstrously false; and would declare its falsity in the fact that, if acted upon, the man would have been left to drown.   In like fashion, to say, *after the event*, that a given idea was true all the time, is to lose sight of what makes an idea an idea, its hypothetical character; and thereby deliberately to transform it into brute dogma—something to which no canon of verification can ever be applied.   The intellectualist almost always treats the pragmatic account as if it were, from the standpoint of the pragmatist as well as from his own, a denial of the existence of truth, while it is nothing but a statement of its nature. When the intellectualist realizes this, he will, I hope, ask himself: What, then, on the pragmatic basis is meant by the proposition that an idea is true all the time?   If the statement that an idea was true all the time has no meaning except that the idea was one which as matter of fact succeeded through action in achieving its intent, mere reiteration that the idea was true all the time or it could not have succeeded, does not take us far.[1]

[1] Such a statement as, for example, Mr. Bradley's (*Mind,* Vol. XIII., No. 51, N.S., p. 3, article on "Truth and Practice") "The idea works . . . but is able to work because I have chosen the right idea" surely loses any argumentative force it may seem to have, when it is recalled that, upon the theory argued against, ability to work and rightness are one and the same thing.   If the wording is changed to read "The idea is able to work because I have chosen an idea which is able to work" the question-begging character of the implied criticism is evident.   The change of phraseology also may suggest the crucial and pregnant question: How does any one know that an idea is able to work excepting by setting it at work?

On the side of things, *reality* is identified with truth; then on the principle that two things that are equal to the same thing are equal to each other, truth as idea and truth as reality are taken to be one and the same thing. Wherever there is an improved or tested idea, an idea which has made good, there is a concrete existence in the way of a completed or harmonized situation. The same activity which proves the idea constructs an inherently satisfied situation out of an inherently dissentient one,—for it is precisely the capacity of the idea as an aim and method of action to determine such transformation that is the criterion of its truth. Now unless all the elements in the situation are held steadily in view, the specific way in which the harmonized reality affords the criterion of truth (namely, through its function of being the last term of a process of active determination) is lost from sight; and the achieved existence in its merely existent character, apart from its practical or fulfilment character, is treated as The Truth. But when the reality is thus separated from the process by which it is achieved, when it is taken just as given, it is neither truth nor a criterion of truth. It is a state of facts like any other. The achieved telephone is a criterion of the validity of a certain prior idea in so far as it is the fulfilment of activities that embody the nature of that idea, but just as telephone, as a machine actually in existence, it is no more truth nor criterion of truth than is a crack in the wall or a cobble-stone on the street.

The intervening term that mediates and completes the confusion of truth with ideas on one hand and " reality " on the other, is, I think, the fact that ideas after they have been tested in action are employed in the development and grounding of further beliefs. There are cases in which an idea ceases to exist as idea as soon as it is made true; this is so as matter of fact and it is impossible to conceive any reason why it should not be so in point of theory. Such is the case, I take it, with a large part—possibly the major portion—of the ideas that mediate the smaller and transient crises of daily practice. I cannot imagine the situation in which the truth to which I have referred above— the verification of a certain idea about a certain noise—would ever function again as truth—save as I have given it a function in this paper by using it as a corroboration of a certain theory. Such ideas mostly cease, giving way to a matter-of-fact status: say, the perception of the noisy street-car. One at the time may say " My idea regarding that noise was a true idea "; or one may not even go so far as that, he may just stop with the eventual perception. But the tested idea need not ever recur as a factor of proof in any other problem. Such, however, is conspicuously not the case with our scientific ideas. In its first value, the idea or hypothesis of gravitation entertained by Newton, stood, when verified, on exactly the same level as the hypothesis regarding the noise in the street. Theoretically, that truth might have been so isolated that its truth character would disappear from thought as soon as a certain factual condition was ascertained. But practically quite the opposite has happened. The idea operates in many other inquiries, and operates no longer as mere idea, but as *proved* idea. Such truths get an " eternal " status—one irrespective of application just now and here, because there are so many nows and heres in which they are useful. Just as to say an idea was true all the time is a way of saying *in retrospect* that it has come out in a certain fashion, so to say that an idea is " eternally true " is to indicate *prospective* modes of application which are indefinitely anticipated. Its meaning, therefore, is strictly pragmatic. It does not indicate a property inherent in the idea as intellectualized existence, but denotes a property of use and employment. Always at hand when needed is a good enough eternal for reasonably minded persons.

IV

I have gone from the very general considerations which occupied us in the earlier portions of this article to matters which relatively at least are specific. I conclude with a summary in the hope that it may bind together the earlier and the later parts of this paper.

1. The condition which antecedes and provokes any particular exercise of reflective knowing is always one of discrepancy, struggle, " collision." This condition is practical, for it involves the habits and interests of the organism, an agent. This does not mean that the struggle is merely personal, or subjective, or psychological. The agent or individual is one factor in the situation—not the situation something subsisting in the individual. The individual has to be identified in the situation, before any situation can be referred—as in psychology—to the individual. But the discrepancy calls out and controls reflective knowing only as the fortunes of an agent are implicated in the crisis. Certain elements stand out as obstacles, as interferences, as deficiencies—in short as unsatisfactory and as requiring something for their completion. Other elements stand out as wanted—as required, as a satisfaction which does not exist. This clash (an accompaniment of all desire) between the given and the wanted, between the pres-

ent and the absent, is at once the root and the
type of that peculiar paradoxical relation between
existence and meaning which Bradley insists upon
as the essence of judgment. It is not irrational
in the sense that we are dealing with appearance
wholesale, but it is non-rational—an evidence that
we are dealing with a practical affair.

2. The intellectual or reflective and logical is a
statement of this conflict: an attempt to describe
and define it. It is, as it were, the practical clash
held off at arm's length for inspection and investigation. In this way brute blind reaction
against the unsatisfactoriness of the situation is
suspended. Action is turned into the channel of
observing, of inferring, of reasoning, or defining
means and end. It is this change in the quality
of activity, from directly overt, to indirect, or inquiring with view to stating, that constitutes the
specific nature of reflective practice to which Mr.
Bradley calls attention. The discovery of the nature of the conflict supplies materials for the fact
or existence side of the judgment. The conception or projection of the object in which the conflict would be terminated furnishes material for
the meaning side of the judgment. It is ideal
because anticipatory, just as the fact side is
existential, because reminiscent or recording.
Hence the two are necessarily both distinguished from and yet referred to each other: only

through location of a problem can a solution be conceived; only in reference to the intent of finding a solution can the elements of a problem be selected and interpreted. In origin and in destiny, this correlative determination of existence and meaning is tentative and experimental. The aim of the subject of the judgment is not to include all possible reality, but to select those elements of a reality that are useful in locating the source and nature of the difficulty in hand. The aim of the predicate is not to bunch all possible meaning and refer it in one final act indiscriminately to all existence, but to state the standpoint and method through which the difficulty of the particular situation may most effectively be dealt with. The selection of what is relevant to the characterization of the problem and the projection of the method of dealing with it are theoretic, hypothetic, intellectual:—that is, they are tentative ways of viewing the matter for the sake of guiding, economizing, and freeing the activities through which it may *really* be dealt with.

3. The criterion of the worth of the idea is thus the capacity of the idea (as a definition of the end or outcome in terms of what is likely to be serviceable as a method) to operate in fulfilling the object for the sake of which it was projected. Capacity of operation in this fashion is the test, measure, or criterion of truth. Hence the criterion is practi-

cal in the most overt sense of that term. We
may, if we choose, regard the object in which the
idea terminates through its use in guiding action,
as the criterion; but if we so choose, it is at our
peril that we forget that this object serves as
criterion in its capacity of fulfilment and not as
sheer objective existence.

4. Difficulties overlap; problems recur which re-
semble each other in the kind of treatment they
demand for solution. Various modes of activity
with their respective ends, going on at some time
more or less independently, get organized into
single comprehensive systems of behavior. The solution of one problem is found to create difficulties
elsewhere; or the truth that is made in the solution of one problem is found to afford an effective
method of dealing with questions arising apparently from unallied sources. Thus certain tested
ideas in performing a constant or recurrent function secure a certain permanent status. The prospective use of such truths, the satisfaction that
we anticipate in their employ, the assurance of
control that we feel in their possession, becomes
relatively much more important than the circumstances under which they were first made true. In
becoming permanent resources, such tested ideas
get a generalized energy of position. They are
truths in general, truths " in themselves " or in the
abstract, truths to which positive value is assigned

on their own account. Such truths are the " eternal truths " of current discussion. They naturally and properly add to their intellectual and to their practical worth a certain esthetic quality. They are interesting to contemplate, and their contemplation arouses emotions of admiration and reverence. To make these emotions the basis of assigning peculiar inherent sanctity to them apart from their warrant in use, is simply to give way to that mood which in primitive man is the cause of attributing magical efficacy to physical things. Esthetically such truths are more than instrumentalities. But to ignore both the instrumental and the esthetic aspect, and to ascribe values due to an instrumental and esthetic character to some interior and *a priori* constitution of truth is to make fetishes of them.

We may not exaggerate the permanence and stability of such truths with respect to their recurring and prospective use. It is only relatively that they are unchanging. When applied to new cases, used as resources for coping with new difficulties, the oldest of truths are to some extent remade. Indeed it is only through such application and such remaking that truths retain their freshness and vitality. Otherwise they are relegated to faint reminiscences of an antique tradition. Even the truth that two and two make four has gained a new meaning, has had its truth in some degree remade, in the development of the modern theory of number. If we put ourselves in the attitude of a scientific inquirer in asking what is the meaning of truth *per se*, there spring up before us those ideas which are actively employed in the mastery of new fields, in the organization of new materials. This is the essential difference between truth and dogma; between the living and the dead and decaying. Above all, it is in the region of moral truth that this perception stands out. Moral truths that are not recreated in application to the urgencies of the passing hour, no matter how true in the place and time of their origin, are pernicious and misleading, *i.e.*, false. And it is perhaps through emphasizing this fact, embodied in one form or another in every system of morals and in every religion of moral import, that one most readily realizes the character of truth.

A SHORT CATECHISM CONCERNING TRUTH [1]

PUPIL. I am desirous, respected teacher, of forming an independent judgment concerning the novel theory of truth that you are said to profess. My eagerness is whetted because the theory as expounded to me by my old teacher, Professor Purus Intellectus, so obviously contravenes common sense, science, and philosophy that I do not understand how it can be advanced in good faith by any reasonable man.

Teacher. As you are already somewhat acquainted with the theory (or at least with what it purports to be), perhaps if you will set forth in order your objections, it will appear that the theory that you are acquainted with is not advanced by any reasonable persons, and that by understanding the theory as it is you will also be led to embrace it.

Pupil: 'Objection One. Pragmatism makes truth a subjective affair, namely the satisfaction afforded individuals by ideas, while everybody

[1] A paper read in the spring of 1909 before the Philosophical Club of Smith College and not previously published.

154

knows that the truth of ideas depends upon their relation to things.

Teacher: Reply. If I were to reply that I hold to existences independent of ideas, existences prior to, synchronous with, and subsequent to ideas, that might seem to you to express only my personal opinion and to have no logical connection with pragmatism. So I beg to remind you that, according to pragmatism, ideas (judgments and reasonings being included for convenience in this term) are attitudes of response taken toward extra-ideal, extra-mental things. Instinct and habit express, for instance, modes of response, but modes inadequate for a progressive being, or for adaptation to an environment presenting novel and unmastered features. Under such conditions, ideas are their surrogates. The origin of an idea is thus in some empirical, extra-mental situation which provokes ideas as modes of response, while their meaning is found in the modifications—the " differences "—they make in this extra-mental situation. Their validity is in turn measured by their capacity to effect the transformation they intend. Origin, content, and value—all alike are extra-ideational. The satisfaction upon which the pragmatist dwells is just the better adjustment of living beings to their environment effected by transformations of the environment through forming and applying ideas.

Pupil: Objection Two. But, as I understand it and as you have yourself confessed in your language, these external things, while they may be external to the particular idea in question, are *empirical;* they are just other experiences and so mental after all.   You hold, I have been informed, that truth is an *experienced* relation, instead of a relation between experience and what transcends it; why then be mealy-mouthed (pardon my eagerness if it leads me astray) in admitting that the whole business is intra-mental?

Teacher: Reply. Your objection combines and confuses two things. To disentangle them is to answer the objection.   (1) The notion of transcendence has a double meaning; first, it denotes that which lies inherently and essentially beyond experience. It is interesting to note that the opponents of pragmatism have been forced by the exigencies of their hostility to resuscitate a doctrine supposedly dead: the doctrine of unexperienceable, unknowable " Things in Themselves." And as if this were not enough, they identify Truth with relationship to this unknowable.   Thereby in behalf of the notion of Truth in general, they land in scepticism with reference to the possibility of any truth in particular.   The pragmatist *is* bound to deny *such* transcendence.   (2) That he is thereby landed in pure subjectivism or the reduction of every existence to the purely mental, follows only if experience means only mental states. The critic appears to hold the Humian doctrine that experience is made up of states of mind, of sensations and ideas. It is then for *him* to decide how, on *his* basis, he escapes subjective idealism, or " mentalism." The pragmatist starts from a much more commonplace notion of experience, that of the plain man who never dreams that to experience a thing is first to destroy the thing and then to substitute a mental state for it. More particularly, the pragmatist has insisted that experience is a matter of functions and habits, of active adjustments and re-adjustments, of co-ordinations and activities, rather than of states of consciousness. To criticise the pragmatist by reading into him exactly the notion of experience that he denies and replaces, may be psychological and unregenerately " pragmatic," but it is hardly " intellectual."

Pupil: Objection Three. You remind me, curiously enough, of a contention of my old instructor to the effect that the pragmatist, when criticised, always shifts his ground. To avoid solipsism and subjectivism, he falls back on things independent of ideas, adducing them in order to pass upon the truth or falsity of the latter. But thereby he only covertly recognizes the intellectualistic standard. Thus he swings unevenly between a denial of science and a clamorous reiteration, in new phraseology, of what all philosophers hold.

Teacher: Reply. Your words have indeed a familiar sound. Apparently, the average intellectualist has got so accustomed to taking truth as a Relation at Large, without specification or analysis, that any attempt at a concrete statement of just what the relationship is appears to be a denial of the relation itself; in which case, he interprets an occasional reminder from the pragmatist that the latter is, after all, attempting to specify the nature of the relation, to be a surrender of the pragmatist's own case, since it admits after all that there is some relation!

However that may be, the pragmatist holds that the relation in question is one of correspondence between existence and thought; but he holds that correspondence instead of being an ultimate and unanalyzable mystery, to be defined by iteration, is precisely a matter of cor-respondence in its plain, familiar sense. A condition of dubious and conflicting tendencies calls out thinking as a method of handling it. This condition produces its own appropriate consequences, bearing its own fruits of weal and woe. The thoughts, the estimates, intents, and projects it calls out, just because they are attitudes of response and of attempted adjustment (*not* mere " states of consciousness "), produce their effects also. The kind of interlocking, of interadjustment that then occurs between these two sorts of consequences constitutes the correspondence that makes truth, just as failure to respond to each other, to work together, constitutes mistake and error—mishandling and wandering. This account may, of course, be wrong—may involve a maladjustment of consequences—but the error in the account, if it exists, must be specific and empirical, and cannot be located by general epistemological accusations.

Pupil: Objection Four. Well, even admitting this version of pragmatism, you cannot deny it still contravenes common sense; for, according to you, the correspondence that constitutes truth does not exist till *after* ideas have worked, while common sense perceives and knows that it is the antecedent agreement of the ideas with reality that enables them to work. If you make the truth of the existence of a Carboniferous age, or the landing of Columbus in 1492, depend upon a future working of an idea about them, you commit yourself to the most fantastic of philosophies.

Teacher: Reply. May I recall to your attention the accusation of " shifting ground " when hard pressed? The intellectualist began, if I remember correctly, with conceiving truth as a relation of thought and existence; has he not, in your last objection, substituted for this conception an identification of the bare existence or event with truth? Which does he mean? How will he have it? The existence of the Carboniferous age, the discovery of America by Columbus are not truths; they are events. Some conviction, some belief, some judgment with reference to them is necessary to introduce the category of truth and falsity. And since the conviction, the judgment, is as matter of fact subsequent to the event, how can its truth consist in the kind of blank, wholesale relationship the intellectualist contends for? How can the present belief jump out of its present skin, dive into the past, and land upon just the one event (that *as* past is gone forever) which, by definition, constitutes its truth? I do not wonder the intellectualist has much to say about " transcendence " when he comes to dealing with the truth of judgments about the past; but why does he not tell us how we manage to know when one thought lands straight on the devoted head of something past and gone, while another thought comes down on the wrong thing in the past?

Pupil. Well, of course, knowledge of the past is very mysterious, but how is the pragmatist any better off?

Teacher. The reply to that may be inferred from what has already been said. The past event has left effects, consequences, that are present and that will continue in the future. Our belief about it, if genuine, must also modify action in *some* way and so have objective effects. If these two sets of effects interlock harmoniously, then the judgment is true. If perchance the past event had no discoverable consequences or our thought of it can work out to no assignable difference anywhere, then there is no possibility of genuine judgment.

Pupil. You have, perhaps, anticipated my next objection, which was that upon the pragmatic theory (by which truth is constituted by future consequences) there are no truths about what is past and gone, since in respect to that ideas can make no difference. For, I suppose, you would say that the difference made is in the effects that continue, since ideas may work out to facilitate or to confuse our relations to these effects. Nevertheless, I am not quite satisfied. For when I say it is true that it rained yesterday, surely the object of my judgment is something past, not future, while pragmatism makes all objects of judgment future.

Teacher: Reply. You confuse the content of a judgment with the *reference* of that content. The content of any idea about yesterday's rain certainly involves past time, but the distinctive or characteristic aim of judgment is none the less to give this content a future reference and function.

Pupil: Objection Five. But your argument requires an absurd identification of truth and verification. To verify ideas is to find out that they were already true; or possessed of the truth relation prior to its discovery in verification.   But the pragmatist holds that the act of finding out that ideas are true creates the thing that is found. In short, you confuse the psychology of finding out with the reality found out.

Teacher: Reply. Many intellectualists have now gone so far as to admit that *verification* is the testing of a judgment by the consequence it imports, the difference it makes—its working. But they still deny any organic connection between the " antecedent " truth property of ideas and the verification (or " making true ") process.   Surely they admit either too much or too little.   (i) If an idea about a past event is already true because of some mysterious static correspondence that it possesses to that past event, how in the world can its truth be *proved* by the *future consequences* of that idea?   Why is it that the intellectualist has not produced any positive theory about the relation of verification to his notion of truth? (ii) Moreover, if verification consists in the experimental working out of a belief, the intellectualist thereby admits that his *own* theory of truth can be *known* to be true only as it is verified by its workings.   But if the theory that truth is a ready-made static property of judgments *is* true, how in the world *can* it be verified by making any specific differences in the course of events?   Every-

where we have to proceed *as if* the pragmatic
theory were the right one. (iii) If he admits
that the pragmatic theory of verification is true,
what meaning remains to the statement that the
idea had the truth property in advance? Why,
simply that it had the property of *ability to work*
—an ability revealed by its actual working. How
can a given fact be an objection to the pragmatic
theory when that fact has a definitely assignable
meaning on the pragmatic theory, while upon the
anti-pragmatic theory it just has to be accepted
as an ultimate, unanalyzable fact?

As to your remark about verification being
merely psychological, I have something to say.
Colleagues of mine are steadily at work in various
laboratories on various researches, forming
hypotheses, experimenting, testing, corroborating,
refuting, modifying ideas. One of them, for example, recently put an immense pendulum in place
in order to repeat and test Foucault's experiment
with reference to the earth's rotation. Do you regard such verification processes as merely psychological?

Pupil. I don't know. Why do you ask?

Teacher. Because if the objector means that
such experimental provings are *merely* psychological, he has of course relegated to the merely psychological (wherever that may be) all the technique of all the physical sciences—a rather high

price to pay for the confutation of the pragmatist. The intellectualist is thus in the dilemma either of conceding to the pragmatist the whole sphere of concrete scientific logic or else of himself regarding all science as merely subjective? Which horn does he choose?

Pupil: Objection Six. I noticed a moment ago that you spoke of the pragmatic theory of truth being true. Surely the pragmatist does not live up to his reputation of having a sense of humor when he claims assent to his theory on the ground that it is true. What is this but to admit intellectualism?

Teacher: Reply. My son, we are evidently nearing the end. Naturally, the pragmatist claims his theory to be true in the pragmatic sense of truth: it works, it clears up difficulties, removes obscurities, puts individuals into more experimental, less dogmatic, and less arbitrarily sceptical relations to life; aligns philosophic with scientific method; does away with self-made problems of epistemology; clarifies and reorganizes logical theory, etc. He is quite content to have the truth of his theory consist in its working in these various ways, and to leave to the intellectualist the proud possession of a static, unanalyzable, unverifiable, unworking property.

Pupil: Objection Seven. Nevertheless, the pragmatist is always appealing to the judgments of

others to corroborate his own judgment.   Surely
this admits the principle of a judgment that is
correct, true, *in se*.

Teacher: Reply.   The pragmatist says that
judgment *is* pragmatic, *i.e.*, originated under conditions of need for a survey and statement, and
tested by efficiency in meeting this need.   And
then you think you have refuted him by saying
that any appeal to judgment is intellectualistic!
Such begging of the question convinces me that
the radical difficulty of the intellectualist is that
he conceives of the pragmatist as beginning with
a theory of truth, when in reality the latter begins
with a theory about judgments and meanings of
which the theory of truth is a corollary.

Pupil: Objection Eight.   Nevertheless, you are
endeavoring to convert your opponent to a certain
theory.   Surely that is an intellectual undertaking, and in theory (at least) the theoretical criterion, as Mr. Bradley has well said, must be
supreme.

Teacher: Reply.   A little reflection will convince
you that you are going around in the same old
circle.   Since men have to act together, since the
individual subsists in social bonds and activities,
to convert another to a certain way of looking
at things is to make social ties and functions better
adapted, more prosperous in their workings.   Only
if the pragmatist held the *intellectualist's* position,

would he appeal to other than what is ultimately a practical need and a practical criterion in endeavoring to convert others.

Pupil: Objection Nine. Still the pragmatic criterion, being satisfactory working, is purely personal and subjective. Whatever works so as to please me is true. Either this is your result (in which case your reference to social relations only denotes at bottom a *number* of purely subjectivistic satisfactions) or else you unconsciously assume an intellectual department of our nature that has to be satisfied; and whose satisfaction is truth. Thereby you admit the intellectualistic criterion.

Teacher: Reply. We seem to have got back to our starting-point, the nature of satisfaction. The intellectualist seems to think that because the pragmatist insists upon the factor of human want, purpose, and realization in the making and testing of judgments, the impersonal factor is therefore denied. But what the pragmatist does is to insist that the human factor must work itself out in *co-operation* with the environmental factor, and that their co-adaptation *is* both " correspondence " and " satisfaction." As long as the human factor is ignored and denied, or is regarded as *merely* psychological (whatever, once more, that means), this human factor will assert itself in irresponsible ways. So long as, particularly in philosophy, a flagrantly unchastened pragmatism reigns, we

shall find, as at present, the most ambitious intellectualistic systems accepted simply because of the
personal comfort they yield those who contrive
and accept them.   Once recognize the human factor, and pragmatism is at hand to insist that the
believer must accept the full consequences of his
beliefs, and that his beliefs must be tried out,
through acting upon them, to discover what is
their meaning or consequence.   Till so tested, he
insists that beliefs, no matter how noble and seemingly edifying, are dogmas, not truths.   Till the
testing has been worked out very completely and
patiently, he holds his beliefs as but provisional,
as working hypotheses, as methods:—and he recognizes the probability that, as additional modes of
testing develop, more and more so-called truths
will be relegated to the category of working hypotheses—till the dogmatic mind is crowded out and
starved out.   At present, the ignoring by philosophers of the part played by personal education,
temperament, and preference in their philosophies
is the chief source of pretentiousness and insin-
cerity in their systems, and is the ground of the
popular disregard for them.

Pupil.   What you say calls to mind something
of Chesterton's that I read recently: " I agree with
the pragmatists that apparent objective truth is
not the whole matter; that there is an authoritative
need to believe the things that are necessary to

the human mind. But I say that one of those necessities precisely is a belief in objective truth. Pragmatism is a matter of human needs and one of the first of human needs is to be something more than a pragmatist." You would say, if I understand you aright, that to fall back upon a supposed necessity of the " human mind " to believe in certain absolute truths, is to evade a proper demand for testing the human mind and all its works.

Teacher. My son, I am glad to leave the last word with you. This *enfant terrible* of intellectualism has revealed that the chief objection of absolutists to the pragmatic doctrine of the personal (or " subjective ") factor in belief is that the pragmatist has spilled the personal milk in the absolutist's cocoanut.

BELIEFS AND EXISTENCES [1]

I

BELIEFS look both ways, towards persons and toward things. They are the original Mr. Facing-both-ways. They form or judge—justify or condemn—the agents who entertain them and who insist upon them. They are of things whose immediate meanings form their content. To believe is to ascribe value, impute meaning, assign import. The collection and interaction of these appraisals and assessments is the world of the common man,—that is, of man as an individual and not as a professional being or class specimen. Thus things are characters, not mere entities; they

[1] Read as the Presidential Address at the fifth annual meeting of the American Philosophical Association, at Cambridge, December 28, 1905, and reprinted with verbal revisions from the *Philosophical Review,* Vol. XV., March, 1906. The substitution of the word "Existences" for the word "Realities" (in the original title) is due to a subsequent recognition on my part that the eulogistic historic associations with the word "Reality" (against which the paper was a protest) infected the interpretation of the paper itself, so that the use of some more colorless word was desirable.

behave and respond and provoke.   In the behavior
that exemplifies and tests their character, they
help and hinder; disturb and pacify; resist and
comply; are dismal and mirthful, orderly and
deformed, queer and commonplace; they agree and
disagree; are better and worse.

Thus the human world, whether or no it have
core and axis, has presence and transfiguration.
It means here and now, not in some transcendent
sphere.   It moves, of itself, to varied incremental
meaning, not to some far off event, whether divine
or diabolic.   Such movement constitutes conduct,
for conduct is the working out of the commitments
of belief.   That believed better is held to, asserted,
affirmed, acted upon.   The moments of its crucial
fulfilment are the natural " transcendentals "; the
decisive, the critical, standards of further estima-
tion, selection, and rejection.   That believed worse
is fled, resisted, transformed into an instrument for
the better.   Characters, in being condensations of
belief, are thus at once the reminders and the
prognostications of weal and woe; they concrete
and they regulate the terms of effective apprehension and appropriation of things.   This general
regulative function is what we mean in calling
them characters, forms.

For beliefs, made in the course of existence,
reciprocate by making existence still farther, by
developing it.   Beliefs are not made *by* existence

in a mechanical or logical or psychological sense. "Reality" naturally instigates belief. It appraises itself and through this self-appraisal manages its affairs. As things are surcharged valuations, so "consciousness" means ways of believing and disbelieving. It is interpretation; not merely existence aware of itself as fact, but existence discerning, judging itself, approving and disapproving.

This double outlook and connection of belief, its implication, on one side, with beings who suffer and endeavor, and, its complication on the other, with the meanings and worths of things, is its glory or its unpardonable sin. We cannot keep connection on one side and throw it away on the other. We cannot preserve significance and decline the personal attitude in which it is inscribed and operative, any more than we can succeed in making things "states" of a "consciousness" whose business is to be an interpretation of things. Beliefs are personal affairs, and personal affairs are adventures, and adventures are, if you please, shady. But equally discredited, then, is the universe of meanings. For the world has meaning as somebody's, somebody's at a juncture, taken for better or worse, and you shall not have completed your metaphysics till you have told whose world is meant and how and what for—in what bias and to what effect. Here is a cake that is had only by eating it, just as there is digestion only *for* life as well as *by* life.

So far the standpoint of the common man. But the professional man, the philosopher, has been largely occupied in a systematic effort to discredit the standpoint of the common man, that is, to disable belief as an ultimately valid principle. Philosophy is shocked at the frank, almost brutal, evocation of beliefs by and in natural existence, like witches out of a desert heath—at a mode of production which is neither logical, nor physical, nor psychological, but just natural, empirical. For modern philosophy is, as every college senior recites, epistemology; and epistemology, as perhaps our books and lectures sometimes forget to tell the senior, has absorbed Stoic dogma. Passionless imperturbability, absolute detachment, complete subjection to a ready-made and finished reality— physical it may be, mental it may be, logical it may be—is its professed ideal. Forswearing the reality of affection, and the gallantry of adventure, the genuineness of the incomplete, the tentative, it has taken an oath of allegiance to Reality, objective, universal, complete; made perhaps of atoms, perhaps of sensations, perhaps of logical meanings. This ready-made reality, already including everything, must of course swallow and absorb belief, must produce it psychologically, mechanically, or logically, according to its own nature; must in any case, instead of acquiring aid and support from belief, resolve it into one of its own preordained creatures, making a desert and calling it harmony, unity, totality.[1]

Philosophy has dreamed the dream of a knowledge which is other than the propitious outgrowth of beliefs that shall develop aforetime their ulterior implications in order to recast them, to rectify their errors, cultivate their waste places, heal their diseases, fortify their feeblenesses:—the dream of a knowledge that has to do with objects having no nature save to be known.

Not that their philosophers have admitted the concrete realizability of their scheme. On the

[1] Since writing the above I have read the following words of a candidly unsympathetic friend of philosophy: " Neither philosophy nor science can institute man's relation to the universe, because such reciprocity must have existed before any kind of science or philosophy can begin; since each investigates phenomena by means of the intellect, and independent of the position and feeling of the investigator; whereas the relation of man to the universe is defined, not by the intellect alone, but by his sensitive perception aided by all his spiritual powers. However much one may assure and instruct a man that all real existence is an idea, that matter is made up of atoms, that the essence of life is corporality or will, that heat, light, movement, electricity, are different manifestations of one and the same energy, one cannot thereby explain to a being with pains, pleasures, hopes, and fears his position in the universe." Tolstoi, essay on " Religion and Morality," in " Essays, Letters, and Miscellanies."

contrary, the assertion of the absolute " Reality " of what is empirically unrealizable is a part of the scheme; the ideal of a universe of pure, cognitional objects, fixed elements in fixed relations. Sensationalist and idealist, positivist and transcendentalist, materialist and spiritualist, defining this object in as many differing ways as they have different conceptions of the ideal and method of knowledge, are at one in their devotion to an identification of Reality with something that connects monopolistically with passionless knowledge, belief purged of all personal reference, origin, and outlook.[1]

What is to be said of this attempt to sever the cord which naturally binds together personal attitudes and the meaning of things? This much at least: the effort to extract meanings, values, from the beliefs that ascribe them, and to give the former absolute metaphysical validity while the latter are sent to wander as scapegoats in the wil-

[1] Hegel may be excepted from this statement. The habit of interpreting Hegel as a Neo-Kantian, a Kantian enlarged and purified, is a purely Anglo-American habit. This is no place to enter into the intricacies of Hegelian exegesis, but the subordination of both logical meaning and of mechanical existence to *Geist,* to life in its own developing movement, would seem to stand out in any unbiased view of Hegel. At all events, I wish to recognize my own personal debt to Hegel for the view set forth in this paper, without, of course, implying that it represents Hegel's own intention.

derness of mere phenomena, is an attempt, which, as long as " our interest's on the dangerous edge of things," will attract an admiring, even if suspicious, audience. Moreover, we may admit that the attempt to catch the universe of immediate experience, of action and passion, coming and going, to damn it in its present body in order expressly to glorify its spirit to all eternity, to validate the meaning of beliefs by discrediting their natural existence, to attribute absolute worth to the intent of human convictions just because of the absolute worthlessness of their content—that the performance of this feat of virtuosity has developed philosophy to its present wondrous, if formidable, technique.

But can we claim more than a *succès d'estime?* Consider again the nature of the effort. The world of immediate meanings, of the world empirically sustained in beliefs, is to be sorted out into two portions, metaphysically discontinuous, one of which shall alone be good and true " Reality," the fit material of passionless, beliefless knowledge; while the other part, that which is excluded, shall be referred exclusively to belief and treated as mere appearance, purely subjective, impressions or effects in consciousness, or as that ludicrously abject modern discovery—an epiphenomenon. And this division into the real and the unreal is accomplished by the very individual whom his own "absolute" results reduce to phenomenality, in terms of the very immediate experience which is infected with worthlessness, and on the basis of preference, of selection that are declared to be unreal! Can the thing be done?

Anyway, the snubbed and excluded factor may always reassert itself. The very pushing it out of "Reality" may but add to its potential energy, and invoke a more violent recoil. When affections and aversions, with the beliefs in which they record themselves and the efforts they exact, are reduced to epiphenomena, dancing an idle attendance upon a reality complete without them, to which they vainly strive to accommodate themselves by mirroring, then may the emotions flagrantly burst forth with the claim that, as a friend of mine puts it, reason is *only* a fig leaf for *their* nakedness. When one man says that need, uncertainty, choice, novelty, and strife have no place in Reality, which is made up wholly of established things behaving by foregone rules, then may another man be provoked to reply that all such fixities, whether named atoms or God, whether they be fixtures of a sensational, a positivistic, or an idealistic system, have existence and import only in the problems, needs, struggles, and instrumentalities of conscious agents and patients. For home rule may be found in the unwritten efficacious constitution of experience.

That contemporaneously we are in the presence of such a reaction is apparent. Let us, in pursuit of our topic, inquire how it came about and why it takes the form that it takes. This consideration may not only occupy the hour, but may help diagram some future parallelogram of forces. The account calls for some sketching (1) of the historical tendencies which have shaped the situation in which a Stoic theory of knowledge claims metaphysical monopoly, and (2) of the tendencies that have furnished the despised principle of belief opportunity and means of reassertion.

II

Imagination readily travels to a period when a gospel of intense, and, one may say, deliberate passionate disturbance appeared to be conquering the Stoic ideal of passionless reason; when the demand for individual assertion by faith against the established, embodied objective order was seemingly subduing the idea of the total subordination of the individual to the universal. By what course of events came about the dramatic reversal, in which an ethically conquered Stoicism became the conqueror, epistemologically, of Christianity?

How are our imaginations haunted by the idea of what might have happened if Christianity had

found ready to its hand intellectual formulations corresponding to its practical proclama-
tions!

That the ultimate principle of conduct is affectional and volitional; that God is love; that access
to the principle is by faith, a personal attitude;
that belief, surpassing logical basis and warrant,
works out through its own operation its own fulfilling evidence: such was the implied moral metaphysic of Christianity. But this implication needed
to become a theory, a theology, a formulation;
and in this need, it found no recourse save to
philosophies that had identified true existence with
the proper object of logical reason. For, in
Greek thought, after the valuable meanings, the
meanings of industry and art that appealed to sustained and serious choice, had given birth and
status to reflective reason, reason denied its an-
cestry of organized endeavor, and proclaimed itself
in its function of self-conscious logical thought to
be the author and warrant of all genuine things.
Yet how nearly Christianity had found prepared
for it the needed means of its own intellectual
statement! We recall Aristotle's account of moral
knowing, and his definition of man. Man as man,
he tells us, is a principle that may be termed
either desiring thought or thinking desire. Not
as pure intelligence does *man* know, but as an
organization of desires effected through reflection

upon their own conditions and consequences. What if Aristotle had only assimilated his idea of theoretical to his notion of practical knowledge! Because practical thinking was so human, Aristotle rejected it in favor of pure, passionless cognition, something superhuman. Thinking desire is experimental, is tentative, not absolute. It looks to the future and to the past for help in the future. It is contingent, not necessary. It doubly relates to the individual: to the individual thing as experienced by an individual agent; not to the universal. Hence desire is a sure sign of defect, of privation, of non-being, and seeks surcease in something which knows it not. Hence desiring reason culminating in beliefs relating to imperfect existence, stands forever in contrast with passionless reason functioning in pure knowledge, logically complete, of perfect being.

I need not remind you how through Neo-Platonism, St. Augustine, and the Scholastic renaissance, these conceptions became imbedded in Christian philosophy; and what a reversal occurred of the original practical principle of Christianity. Belief is henceforth important because it is the mere antecedent in a finite and fallen world, a temporal and phenomenal world infected with non-being, of true knowledge to be achieved only in a world of completed Being. Desire is but the self-consciousness of defect striving to its own termination in perfect possession, through perfect knowledge of perfect being. I need not remind you that the *prima facie* subordination of reason to authority, of knowledge to faith, in the medieval code, is, after all, but the logical result of the doctrine that man as man (since only reasoning desire) is merely phenomenal; and has his reality in God, who as God is the complete union of rational insight and being—the term of man's desire, and the fulfilment of his feeble attempts at knowing. Authority, " faith " as it then had to be conceived, meant just that this Being comes externally to the aid of man, otherwise hopelessly doomed to misery in long drawn out error and non-being, and disciplines him till, in the next world under more favoring auspices, he may have his desires stilled in good, and his faith may yield to knowledge:—for we forget that the doctrine of immortality was not an appendage, but an integral part of the theory that since knowledge is the *true* function of man, happiness is attained only in knowledge, which itself exists only in achievement of perfect Being or God.

For my part, I can but think that medieval absolutism, with its provision for authoritative supernatural assistance in this world and assertion of supernatural realization in the next, was more logical, as well as more humane, than the modern absolutism, that, with the same logical premises, bids man find adequate consolation and support in

the fact that, after all, his strivings are already
eternally fulfilled, his errors already eternally
transcended, his partial beliefs already eternally
comprehended.

The modern age is marked by a refusal to be
satisfied with the postponement of the exercise and
function of reason to another and supernatural
sphere, and by a resolve to practise itself upon its
present object, nature, with all the joys thereunto
appertaining. The pure intelligence of Aristotle,
thought thinking itself, expresses itself as free
inquiry directed upon the present conditions of its
own most effective exercise. The principle of the
inherent relation of thought to being was preserved intact, but its practical locus was moved
down from the next world to this. Spinoza's
" God or Nature " is the logical outcome; as is also
his strict correlation of the attribute of matter with
the attribute of thought; while his combination
of thorough distrust of passion and faith with
complete faith in reason and all-absorbing passion
for knowledge is so classic an embodiment of the
whole modern contradiction that it may awaken admiration where less thorough-paced formulations
call out irritation.

In the practical devotion of present intelligence
to its present object, nature, science was born,
and also its philosophical counterpart, the theory
of knowledge. Epistemology only generalized in

its loose, although narrow and technical way, the question practically urgent in Europe: How is science possible? How can intelligence actively and directly get at its object?

Meantime, through Protestantism the values, the meanings formerly characterizing the next life (the opportunity for full perception of perfect being), were carried over into present-day emotions and responses.

The dualism between faith authoritatively supported as the principle of this life, and knowledge supernaturally realized as the principle of the next, was transmuted into the dualism between intelligence now and here occupied with natural things, and the affections and accompanying beliefs, now and here realizing spiritual worths. For a time this dualism operated as a convenient division of labor. Intelligence, freed from responsibility for and preoccupation with supernatural truths, could occupy itself the more fully and efficiently with the world that now is; while the affections, charged with the values evoked in the medieval discipline, entered into the present enjoyment of the delectations previously reserved for the saints. Directness took the place of systematic intermediation; the present of the future; the individual's emotional consciousness of the supernatural institution. Between science and faith, thus conceived, a bargain was struck. Hands off; each to his own, was the compact; the natural world to intelligence, the moral, the spiritual world to belief. This (natural) world for knowledge; that (supernatural) world for belief. Thus the antithesis, unexpressed, ignored, *within experience*, between belief and knowledge, between the purely objective values of thought and the personal values of passion and volition, was more fundamental, more determining, than the opposition, explicit and harassing, *within knowledge*, between subject and object, mind and matter.

This latent antagonism worked out into the open. In scientific detail, knowledge encroached upon the historic traditions and opinions with which the moral and religious life had identified itself. It made history to be as natural, as much its spoil, as physical nature. It turned itself upon man, and proceeded remorselessly to account for his emotions, his volitions, his opinions. Knowledge, in its general theory, as philosophy, went the same way. It was pre-committed to the old notion: the absolutely real is the object of *knowledge*, and hence is something universal and impersonal. So, whether by the road of sensationalism or rationalism, by the path of mechanicalism or objective idealism, it came about that concrete selves, specific feeling and willing beings, were relegated with the beliefs in which they declare themselves to the " phenomenal."

III

So much for the situation against which some contemporary tendencies are a deliberate protest.

What of the positive conditions that give us not mere protest, like the unreasoning revolt of heart against head found at all epochs, but something articulate and constructive? The field is only too large, and I shall limit myself to the evolution of the knowledge standpoint itself. I shall suggest, first, that the progress of intelligence directed upon natural materials has evolved a procedure of knowledge that renders untenable the inherited conception of knowledge; and, secondly, that this result is reinforced by the specific results of some of the special sciences.

1. First, then, the very use of the knowledge standpoint, the very expression of the knowledge preoccupation, has produced methods and tests that, when formulated, intimate a radically different conception of knowledge, and of its relation to existence and belief, than the orthodox one.

The one thing that stands out is that thinking is inquiry, and that knowledge as science is the outcome of systematically directed inquiry. For a time it was natural enough that inquiry should be interpreted in the old sense, as just change of subjective attitudes and opinions to make them square up with a " reality " that is already there in ready-made, fixed, and finished form. The rationalist had one notion of the reality, *i.e.*, that it was of the nature of laws, genera, or an ordered system, and so thought of concepts, axioms, etc., as the indicated modes of representation. The empiricist, holding reality to be a lot of little discrete particular lumps, thought of disjointed sensations as its appropriate counterpart. But both alike were thorough conformists. If " reality " is already and completely given, and if knowledge is just submissive acceptance, then, of course, inquiry is only a subjective change in the human " mind " or in " consciousness,"—these being subjective and "unreal."

But the very development of the sciences served to reveal a peculiar and intolerable paradox. Epistemology, having condemned inquiry once for all to the region of subjectivity in an invidious sense, finds itself in flat opposition in principle and in detail to the assumption and to the results of the sciences. Epistemology is bound to deny to the results of the special sciences in detail any ulterior objectivity just because they always *are* in a process of inquiry—*in* solution. While a man may not be halted at being told that his mental activities, since his, are not genuinely real, many men will draw violently back at being told that all the discoveries, conclusions, explanations, and theories of the sciences share the same fate, being the products of a discredited mind.   And, in general, epistemology, in relegating human thinking as inquiry to a merely phenomenal region, makes concrete approximation and conformity to objectivity hopeless. Even if it did square itself up to and by " reality " it never could be sure of it.   The ancient myth of Tantalus and his effort to drink the water before him seems to be ingeniously prophetic of modern epistemology.   The thirstier, the needier of truth the human mind, and the intenser the efforts put forth to slake itself in the ocean of being just beyond the edge of consciousness, the more surely the living waters of truth recede!

When such self-confessed sterility is joined with consistent derogation of all the special results of the special sciences, some one is sure to raise the cry of " dog in the manger," or of " sour grapes."   A revision of the theory of thinking, of inquiry, would seem to be inevitable; a revision which should cease trying to construe knowledge as an attempted approximation to a reproduction of reality under conditions that condemn it in advance to failure; a revision which should start frankly from the fact of thinking as inquiring, and purely external realities as terms in inquiries, and which should construe validity, objectivity, truth, and the test and system of truths, on the basis of what they actually mean and do within inquiry.

Such a standpoint promises ample revenge for

the long damnation and longer neglect to which
the principle of belief has been subjected. The
whole procedure of thinking as developed in those
extensive and intensive inquiries that constitute
the sciences, is but rendering into a systematic
technique, into an art deliberately and delightfully
pursued, the rougher and cruder means by which
practical human beings have in all ages worked
out the implications of their beliefs, tested them,
and endeavored in the interests of economy, efficiency, and freedom, to render them coherent with
one another. Belief, sheer, direct, unmitigated
belief, reappears as the working hypothesis;
action that at once develops and tests belief reappears in experimentation, deduction, demonstration; while the machinery of universals, axioms,
a priori truths, etc., becomes a systematization of
the way in which men have always worked out, in
anticipation of overt action, the implications of
their beliefs, with a view to revising them, in the
interests of obviating unfavorable, and securing
welcome consequences. Observation, with its machinery of sensations, measurements, etc., is the
resurrection of the way in which agents have always
faced and tried to define the problems that face
them; truth is the union of abstract postulated
meanings and of concrete brute facts in a way
that circumvents the latter by judging them from
a new standpoint, while it tests concepts by using

them as methods in the same active experience. It all comes to experience personally conducted and personally consummated.

Let consciousness of these facts dawn a little more brightly over the horizon of epistemological prejudices, and it will be seen that nothing prevents admitting the genuineness both of thinking activities and of their characteristic results, except the notion that belief itself is not a genuine ingredient of existence—a notion which itself is not only a belief, but a belief which, unlike the convictions of the common man and the hypotheses of science, finds its proud proof in the fact that it does not demean itself so unworthily as to work.

Once believe that beliefs themselves are as " real " as anything else can ever be, and we have a world in which uncertainty, doubtfulness, really inhere; and in which personal attitudes and responses are real both in their own distinctive existence, and as the only ways in which an as yet undetermined factor of reality takes on shape, meaning, value, truth.   If " to wilful men the injuries that they themselves procure, must be their schoolmasters "—and all beliefs are wilful—then by the same token the propitious evolutions of meaning, which wilful men secure to an expectant universe, must be their compensation and their justification.   In a doubtful and needy universe elements must be beggarly, and the development

of personal beliefs into experimentally executed
systems of actions, is the organized bureau of
philanthropy which confers upon a travailing universe the meaning for which it cries out. The
apostrophe of the poet is above all to man the
thinker, the inquirer, the knower:

> O Dreamer! O Desirer, goer down
> Unto untraveled seas in untried ships,
> O crusher of the unimagined grape,
> On unconceivèd lips.

2. Biology, psychology, and the social sciences
proffer an imposing body of concrete facts that
also point to the rehabilitation of belief—to the
interpretation of knowledge as a human and practical outgrowth of belief, not to belief as the state
to which knowledge is condemned in a merely finite
and phenomenal world. I need not, as I cannot,
here summarize the psychological revision which
the notions of sensation, perception, conception,
cognition in general have undergone, all to one intent. " Motor " is writ large on their face. The
testimony of biology is unambiguous to the effect
that the organic instruments of the whole intellectual life, the sense-organs and brain and their
connections, have been developed on a definitely
practical basis and for practical aims, for the
purpose of such control over conditions as will
sustain and vary the meanings of life. The his-

toric sciences are equally explicit in their evidence that knowledge as a system of information and instruction is a coöperative social achievement, at all times socially toned, sustained, and directed; and that logical thinking is a reweaving through individual activity of this social fabric at such points as are indicated by prevailing needs and aims.

This bulky and coherent body of testimony is not, of course, of itself philosophy. But it supplies, at all events, facts that have scientific backing, and that are as worthy of regard as the facts pertinent to any science. At the present time these facts seem to have some peculiar claim just because they present traits largely ignored in prior philosophic formulations, while those belonging to mathematics and physics have so largely wrought their sweet will on systems. Again, it would seem as if in philosophies built deliberately upon the knowledge principle, any body of known facts should not have to clamor for sympathetic attention.

Such being the case, the reasons for ruling psychology and sociology and allied sciences out of competency to give philosophic testimony have more significance than the bare denial of jurisdiction. They are evidences of the deep-rooted preconception that whatever concerns a particular conscious agent, a wanting, struggling, satisfied

and dissatisfied being, must of course be only " phenomenal " in import.

This aversion is the more suggestive when the
professed idealist appears as the special champion
of the virginity of pure knowledge. The idealist,
so content with the notion that consciousness determines reality, provided it be done once for all,
at a jump and in lump, is so uneasy in presence
of the idea that empirical conscious beings genuinely determine existences now and here! One is
reminded of the story told, I think, by Spencer.
Some committee had organized and contended,
through a long series of parliaments, for the
passage of a measure. At last one of their meet-
ings was interrupted with news of success. Con-
sternation was the result. What was to become
of the occupation of the committee? So, one asks,
what is to become of idealism at large, of the
wholesale unspecifiable determination of " reality "
by or in " consciousness," if specific conscious beings, John Smiths, and Susan Smiths (to say nothing of their animal relations), beings with bowels
and brains, are found to exercise influence upon
the character and existence of reals?

One would be almost justified in construing
idealism as a Pickwickian scheme, so willing is it to
idealize the principle of intelligence at the expense
of its specific undertakings, were it not that this
reluctance is the necessary outcome of the Stoic

basis and tenor of idealism—its preoccupation with logical contents and relations in abstraction from their *situs* and function in conscious living beings.

IV

I have suggested to you the naïve conception of the relation of beliefs to realities: that beliefs are themselves real without discount, manifesting their reality in the usual proper way, namely, by modifying and shaping the reality of other things, so that they connect the bias, the preferences and affections, the needs and endeavors of personal lives with the values, the characters ascribed to things: —the latter thus becoming worthy of human acquaintance and responsive to human intercourse. This was followed by a sketch of the history of thought, indicating how beliefs and all they insinuate were subjected to preconceived notions of knowledge and of " reality " as a monopolistic possession of pure intellect. Then I traced some of the *motifs* that make for reconsideration of the supposed uniquely exclusive relation of logical knowledge and " reality "; *motifs* that make for a less invidiously superior attitude towards the convictions of the common man.

In concluding, I want to say a word or two to mitigate—for escape is impossible—some misunderstandings. And, to begin with, while possible doubts inevitably troop with actual beliefs, the doctrine in question is not particularly sceptical. The radical empiricist, the humanist, the pragmatist, label him as you will, believes not in fewer but in more " realities " than the orthodox philosophers warrant. He is not concerned, for example, in discrediting objective realities and logical or universal thinking; he is interested in such a reinterpretation of the sort of " reality " which these things possess as will accredit, without depreciation, concrete empirical conscious centers of action and passion.

My second remark is to the opposite effect. The intent is not especially credulous, although it starts from and ends with the radical credulity of all knowledge. To suppose that because the sciences are ultimately instrumental to human beliefs, we are therefore to be careless of the most exact possible use of extensive and systematic scientific methods, is like supposing that because a watch is made to tell present time, and not to be an exemplar of transcendent, absolute time, watches might as well be made of cheap stuffs, casually wrought and clumsily put together. It is the task of telling present time, with all its urgent implications, that brings home, steadies, and enlarges the responsibility for the best possible use of intelligence, the instrument.

For one, I have no interest in the old, old scheme
of derogating from the worth of knowledge in
order to give an uncontrolled field for some *special*
beliefs to run riot in,—be these beliefs even faith
in immortality, in some special sort of a Deity,
or in some particular brand of freedom.   Any one
of our beliefs is subject to criticism, revision, and
even ultimate elimination through the development
of its own implications by intelligently directed
action.   Because reason is a scheme of working out
the meanings of convictions in terms of one another and of the consequences they import in
further experience, convictions are the more, not
the less, amenable and responsible to the full exercise of reason.[1]

Thus we are put on the road to that most de-

---

[1] There will of course come in time with the development
of this point of view an organon of beliefs.   The signs of
a genuine as against a simulated belief will be studied;
belief as a vital personal reaction will be discriminated from
habitual, incorporate, unquestioned (because unconsciously
exercised) traditions of social classes and professions.   In
his "Will to Believe" Professor James has already laid
down two traits of genuine belief (viz., "forced option,"
and acceptance of responsibility for results) which are
almost always ignored in criticisms (really caricatures) of
his position.   In the light of such an organon, one might
come to doubt whether *belief* in, say, immortality (as distinct from hope on one side and a sort of intellectual balance of probability of opinion on the other) can genuinely
exist at all.

sirable thing,—the union of acknowledgment of moral powers and demands with thoroughgoing naturalism. No one really wants to lame man's practical nature; it is the supposed exigencies of natural science that force the hand. No one really bears a grudge against naturalism for the sake of obscurantism. It is the need of some sacred reservation for moral interests that coerces. We all want to be as naturalistic as we can be. But the " can be " is the rub. If we set out with a fixed dualism of belief and knowledge, then the uneasy fear that the natural sciences are going to encroach and destroy " spiritual values " haunts us. So we build them a citadel and fortify it; that is, we isolate, professionalize, and thereby weaken beliefs. But if beliefs are the most natural, and in that sense, the most metaphysical of all things, and if knowledge is an organized technique for working out their implications and interrelations, for directing their formation and employ, how unnecessary, how petty the fear and the caution. Because freedom of belief is ours, free thought may exercise itself; the freer the thought the more sure the emancipation of belief. Hug some special belief and one fears knowledge; believe in belief and one loves and cleaves to knowledge.

We have here, too, the possibility of a common understanding, in thought, in language, in outlook, of the philosopher and the common man. What would not the philosopher give, did he not have to part with some of his common humanity in order to join a class? Does he not always, when challenged, justify himself with the contention that all men naturally philosophize, and that he but does in a conscious and orderly way what leads to harm when done in an indiscriminate and irregular way? If philosophy be at once a natural history *and* a logic—an art—of beliefs, then its technical justification is at one with its human justification. The natural attitude of man, said Emerson, is believing; " the philosopher, after some struggle, having only reasons for believing." Let the struggle then enlighten and enlarge beliefs; let the reasons kindle and engender new beliefs.

Finally, it is not a solution, but a problem which is presented. As philosophers, our disagreements as to conclusions are trivial compared with our disagreement as to problems. To see the problem another sees, in the same perspective and at the same angle—that amounts to something. Agreement in solutions is in comparison perfunctory. To experience the same problem another feels— that perhaps is agreement. In a world where distinctions are as invidious as comparisons are odious, and where intellect works only by comparison and distinction, pray what is one to do?

But beliefs are personal matters, and the person,

we may still believe, is social.   To be a man is to be thinking desire; and the agreement of desires is not in oneness of intellectual conclusion, but in the sympathies of passion and the concords of action: —and yet significant union in affection and behavior may depend upon a consensus in thought that is secured only by discrimination and comparison.

EXPERIENCE AND OBJECTIVE IDEALISM [1]

I

IDEALISM as a philosophic system stands in such a delicate relation to experience as to invite attention. In its subjective form, or sensationalism, it claims to be the last word of empiricism. In its objective, or rational form, it claims to make good the deficiencies of the subjective type, by emphasizing the work of thought that supplies the factors of objectivity and universality lacking in sensationalism. With reference to experience *as it now is*, such idealism is half opposed to empiricism and half committed to it,—antagonistic, so far as existing experience is regarded as tainted with a sensational character; favorable, so far as this experience is even now prophetic of some final, all-comprehensive, or absolute experience, which in truth is one with reality.

That this combination of opposition to present experience with devotion to the cause of experience

---

[1] Reprinted, with slight verbal changes, from the *Philosophical Review*, Vol. XV. (1906).

in the abstract leaves objective idealism in a position of unstable equilibrium from which it can find release only by euthanasia in a thorough-going empiricism seems evident. Some of the reasons for this belief may be readily approached by a summary sketch of three historic episodes in which have emerged important conceptions of experience and its relation to reason. The first takes us to classic Greek thought. Here experience means the preservation, through memory, of the net result of a multiplicity of particular doings and sufferings; a preservation that affords positive skill in maintaining further practice, and promise of success in new emergencies. The craft of the carpenter, the art of the physician are standing examples of its nature. It differs from instinct and blind routine or servile practice because there is some knowledge of materials, methods, and aims, in their adjustment to one another. Yet the marks of its passive, habitual origin are indelibly stamped upon it. On the knowledge side it can never aspire beyond opinion, and if true opinion be achieved, it is only by happy chance. On the active side it is limited to the accomplishment of a special work or a particular product, following some unjustified, because assumed, method. Thus it contrasts with the true knowledge of reason, which is direct apprehension, self-revealing and self-validating, of an eternal and harmonious content. The regions in which

experience and reason respectively hold sway are
thus explained. Experience has to do with production, which, in turn, is relative to decay. It
deals with generation, becoming, not with finality,
being. Hence it is infected with the trait of relative non-being, of mere imitativeness; hence its
multiplicity, its logical inadequacy, its relativity
to a standard and end beyond itself. Reason, *per
contra*, has to do with meaning, with significance
(ideas, forms), that is eternal and ultimate. Since
the meaning of anything is the worth, the good,
the end of that thing, experience presents us with
partial and tentative efforts to achieve the embodiment of purpose, under conditions that doom
the attempt to inconclusiveness. It has, however, its meed of reality in the degree in which
its results *participate* in meaning, the good,
reason.

From this classic period, then, comes the antithesis of experience as the historically achieved
embodiments of meaning, partial, multiple, inse-
cure, to reason as the source, author, and con-
tainer of *meaning*, permanent, assured, unified.
Idealism means ideality, experience means brute
and broken facts. That things exist because of
and for the sake of meaning, and that experience
gives us meaning in a servile, interrupted, and
inherently deficient way—such is the standpoint.
Experience gives us meaning in process of be-

coming; special and isolated instances in which it *happens*, temporally, to appear, rather than meaning pure, undefiled, independent.   Experience presents purpose, the good, struggling against obstacles, "involved in matter."

Just how much the vogue of modern neo-Kantian idealism, professedly built upon a strictly epistemological instead of upon a cosmological basis, is due, in days of a declining theology, to a vague sense that affirming the function of reason in the constitution of a knowable world (which in its own constitution as logically knowable may be, morally and spiritually, anything you please), carries with it an assurance of the superior reality of the good and the beautiful as well as of the " true," it would be hard to say.   Certainly unction seems to have descended upon epistemology, in apostolic succession, from classic idealism; so that neo-Kantianism is rarely without a tone of edification, as if feeling itself the patron of man's spiritual interests in contrast to the supposed crudeness and insensitiveness of naturalism and empiricism.   At all events, we find here one element in our problem: Experience considered as the summary of past episodic adventures and happenings in relation to fulfilled and adequately expressed meaning.

The second historic event centers about the controversy of innate ideas, or pure concepts.   The issue is between empiricism and rationalism as theories of the origin and validation of scientific knowledge. The empiricist is he who feels that the chief obstacle which prevents scientific method from making way is the belief in pure thoughts, not derived from particular observations and hence not responsible to the course of experience. His objection to the " high *a priori* road " is that it introduces in irresponsible fashion a mode of presumed knowledge which may be used at any turn to stand sponsor for mere tradition and prejudice, and thus to nullify the results of science resting upon and verified by observable facts. Experience thus comes to mean, to use the words of Peirce, " that which is forced upon a man's recognition will-he, nill-he, and shapes his thoughts to something quite different from what they naturally would have taken." [1] The same definition is found in James, in his chapter on Necessary Truths: " Experience means experience of something foreign supposed to impress us whether spontaneously or in consequence of our own exertions and acts." [2] As Peirce points out, this notion of experience as the foreign element that forces the hand of thought and controls its efficacy, goes back to Locke. Experience is " observation employed either about external sensible objects, or about the internal operations of our

[1] C. S. Peirce, *Monist*, Vol. XVI., p. 150.
[2] *Psychology*, Vol. II., p. 618.

minds " [1]—as furnishing in short all the valid data and tests of thinking and knowledge. This meaning, thinks Peirce, should be accepted " as a landmark which it would be a crime to disturb or displace."

The contention of idealism, here bound up with rationalism, is that perception and observation cannot guarantee knowledge in its honorific sense (science) ; that the peculiar differentia of scientific knowledge is a constancy, a universality, and necessity that contrast at every point with perceptual data, and that indispensably require the function of conception. [2] In short, *qualitative transformation* of *facts* (data of perception), not their mechanical subtraction and recombination, is the difference between scientific and perceptual knowledge. Here the problem which emerges is, of course, the significance of perception and of conception in respect to experience. [3]

---

[1] " Essay concerning Human Understanding," Book II., Chapter II., § 2. Locke doubtless derived this notion from Bacon.

[2] It is hardly necessary to refer to the stress placed upon mathematics, as well as upon fundamental propositions in logic, ethics, and cosmology.

[3] Of course there are internal historic connections between experience as effective " memory," and experience as " observation." But the motivation and stress, the problem, has quite shifted. It may be remarked that Hobbes still writes under the influence of the Aristotelian conception. " Experience is nothing but Memory " ("Elements of Philosophy," Part I., Chapter I., § 2), and hence is opposed to science.

The third episode reverses in a curious manner (which confuses present discussion) the notion of experience as a foreign, alien, coercive material. It regards experience as a fortuitous association, by merely psychic connections, of individualistic states of consciousness.   This is due to the Humian development of Locke.   The " objects " and " operations," which to Locke were just given and secured in observation, become shifting complexes of subjective sensations and ideas, whose apparent permanency is due to discoverable illusions.   This, of course, is the empiricism which made Kant so uneasily toss in his dogmatic slumbers (a tossing that he took for an awakening); and which, by reaction, called out the conception of thought as a function operating both to elevate perceptual data to scientific status, and also to confer objective status, or knowable character, upon even sensational data and their associative combinations.[1]   Here emerges the third element in our problem: The function of thought as furnishing

[1] There are, of course, anticipations of Hume in Locke. But to regard Lockeian experience as equivalent to Humian is to pervert history.   Locke, as he was to himself and to the century succeeding him, was not a subjectivist, but in the main a common sense objectivist.   It was this that gave him his historic influence.   But so completely has the Hume-Kant controversy dominated recent thinking that it is constantly projected backward.   Within a few weeks I have seen three articles, all insisting that the meaning of the

objectivity to any experience that claims cognitive reference or capacity.

Summing up the matter, idealism stands forth with its assertion of thought or reason as (1) the sponsor for all significance, ideality, purpose, in experience,—the author of the good and the beautiful as well as the true; (2) the power, located in pure conceptions, required to elevate perceptive or observational material to the plane of science; and (3) the constitution that gives objectivity, even the semblance of order, system, connection, mutual reference, to sensory data that without its assistance are mere subjective flux.

term experience must be subjective, and stating or implying that those who take the term objectively are subverters of established usage! But a casual study of the dictionary will reveal that experience has always meant "*what* is experienced," observation as a source of knowledge, as well as the act, fact, or mode of experiencing. In the Oxford Dictionary, the (obsolete) sense of "experimental testing," of actual "observation of facts and events," and "the fact of being consciously affected by an act" have almost contemporaneous datings, viz., 1384, 1377, and 1382 respectively. A usage almost more objective than the second, the Baconian use, is "what has been experienced; the events that have taken place within the knowledge of an individual, a community, mankind at large, either during a particular period or generally." This dates back to 1607. Let us have no more captious criticisms and plaints based on ignorance of linguistic usage. [This pious wish has not been met. J. D., 1909.]

II

I begin the discussion with the last-named function. Thought is here conceived as *a priori*, not in the sense of particular innate ideas, but of a function that constitutes the very possibility of any objective experience, any experience involving reference beyond its own mere subjective happening. I shall try to show that idealism is condemned to move back and forth between two inconsistent interpretations of this *a priori* thought. It is taken to mean both the organized, the regulated, the informed, established character of experience, an order immanent and constitutional; and an agency which organizes, regulates, forms, synthesizes, a power operative and constructive. And the oscillation between and confusion of these two diverse senses is necessary to Neo-Kantian idealism.

When Kant compared his work in philosophy to that of the men who introduced construction into geometry, and experimentation into physics and chemistry, the point of his remarks depends upon taking the *a priori* worth of thought in a regulative, directive, controlling sense, thought as consciously, intentionally, making an experience *different* in a *determinate* sense and manner. But the point of his answer to Hume consists in taking the *a priori* in the other sense, as something which is *already* immanent in *any* experience, and which accordingly makes no determinate difference to any one experience as compared with any other, or with any past or future form of itself. The concept is treated first as that which makes an experience actually different, controlling its evolution towards consistency, coherency, and objective reliability; then, it is treated as that which has already effected the organization of any and every experience that comes to recognition at all. The fallacy from which he never emerges consists in vibrating between the definition of a concept as a rule of constructive synthesis in a *differential* sense, and the definition of it as a static endowment lurking in " mind," and giving automatically a hard and fixed law for the determination of every experienced object. The *a priori* conceptions of Kant as immanent fall, like the rain, upon the just and the unjust; upon error, opinion, and hallucination. But Kant slides into these *a priori* functions the preferential values exercised by empirical reflective thought. The concept of triangle, taken geometrically, means doubtless a determinate method of construing space elements; but to Kant it also means something that exists in the mind *prior* to all such geometrical constructions and that unconsciously lays down the law not only for their conscious elaboration, but also for any space perception, even for that which takes a rectangle to be a triangle.   The first of the meanings is intelligible, and marks a definite contribution to the logic of science.   But it is not " objective idealism "; it is a contribution to a revised empiricism.   The second is a dark saying.

That organization of some sort exists in every experience I make no doubt.   That isolation, discrepancy, the fragmentary, the incompatible, are brought to recognition and to logical function only with reference to some prior existential mode of organization seems clear.   And it seems equally clear that reflection goes on with profit only because the materials with which it deals have already some degree of organization, or exemplify various relationships.   As against Hume, or even Locke, we may be duly grateful to Kant for enforcing acknowledgment of these facts.   But the acknowledgment means simply an improved and revised empiricism.

For, be it noted, this organization, first, is not the work of reason or thought, unless " reason " be stretched beyond all identification; and, secondly, it has no sacrosanct or finally valid and worthful character.   (1) Experience always carries with it and within it certain systematized arrangements, certain classifications (using the term without intellectualistic prejudice), coexistent and serial.   If we attribute these to " thought " then the structure of the brain of a Mozart which hears and combines

sounds in certain groupings, the psycho-physical
visual habit of the Greek, the locomotor apparatus
of the human body in the laying-out and plotting
of space is " thought." Social institutions, established political customs, effect and perpetuate
modes of reaction and of perception that compel
a certain grouping of objects, elements, and values.
A national constitution brings about a definite
arrangement of the factors of human action which
holds even physical things together in certain
determinate orders. Every successful economic
process, with its elaborate divisions and adjustments of labor, of materials and instruments, is
just such an objective organization. Now it is one
thing to say that thought has played a part in
the origin and development of such organizations,
and continues to have a rôle in their judicious employment and application; it is another to say that
these organizations *are* thought, or are its exclusive product. Thought that functions in these
ways is distinctively *reflective* thought, thought as
practical, volitional, deliberately exercised for specific aims—thought as an act, an art of skilled
mediation. As *reflective* thought, its end is to
terminate its own first and experimental forms, and
to secure an organization which, while it may evoke
new reflective thinking, puts an end to the thinking that secured the organization. *As organizations*, as established, effectively controlling ar-

rangements of objects in experience, their mark is that they are not thoughts, but habits, customs of action.[1]

Moreover, such reflective thought as does intervene in the formation and maintenance of these practical organizations harks back to prior practical organizations, biological and social in nature. It serves to *valuate* organizations already existent as biological functions and instincts, while, as itself a biological activity, it redirects them to new conditions and results. Recognize, for example, that a geometric concept is a practical locomotor function of arranging stimuli in reference to maintenance of life activities *brought into consciousness*, and then serving as a center of reorganization of such activities to freer, more varied flexible and valuable forms; recognize this, and we have the truth of the Kantian idea, without its excrescences and miracles. The concept is the practical activity doing consciously and artfully what it had aforetime done blindly and aimlessly, and thereby not only doing it better but opening up a freer world of significant activities. Thought as such a reorganization of natural functions does naturally

---

[1] The relationship of organization and thought is precisely that which we find psychologically typified by the rhythmic functions of habit and attention, attention being always, *ab quo*, a sign of the failure of habit, and, *ad quem*, a reconstructive modification of habit.

what Kantian forms and schematizations do only supernaturally. In a word, the constructive or organizing activity of " thought " does not inhere in thought as a transcendental function, a form or mode of some supra-empirical ego, mind, or consciousness, but in thought as itself vital activity. And in any case we have passed to the idea of thought as reflectively reconstructive and directive, and away from the notion of thought as immanently constitutional and organizational. To make this passage and yet to ignore its existence and import is essential to objective idealism.

(2) No final or ultimate validity attaches to these original arrangements and institutionalizations in any case. Their value is teleological and experimental, not fixedly ontological. " Law and order " are good things, but not when they become rigidity, and create mechanical uniformity or routine. Prejudice is the acme of the *a priori*. Of the *a priori* in this sense we may say what is always to be said of habits and institutions: They are good servants, but harsh and futile masters. Organization as already effected is always in danger of becoming a *mortmain;* it may be a way of sacrificing novelty, flexibility, freedom, creation to static standards. The curious inefficiency of idealism at this point is evident in the fact that genuine thought, empirical reflective thought, is required

precisely for the purpose of re-forming established and set formations.

In short, (*a*) *a priori* character is no exclusive function of thought. Every biological function, every motor attitude, every vital impulse as the carrying vehicle of experience is thus *apriorily* regulative in prospective reference; what we call apperception, expectation, anticipation, desire, demand, choice, are pregnant with this constitutive and organizing power. (*b*) **In so far as** " thought " does exercise such reorganizing power, it is because thought is itself still a *vital* function. (*c*) Objective idealism depends not only upon ignoring the existence and capacity of vital functions, but upon a profound confusion of the constitutional *a priori*, the unconsciously dominant, with empirically reflective thought. In the sense in which the *a priori* is worth while as an attribute of thought, thought cannot be what the objective idealist defines it as being. Plain, ordinary, everyday empirical reflections, operating as centers of inquiry, of suggestion, of experimentation, exercise the valuable function of regulation, in an auspicious direction, of subsequent experiences.

The categories of accomplished systematization cover alike the just and the unjust, the false and the true, while (unlike God's rain) they exercise no *specific* or *differential* activity of stimulation and control. Error and inefficiency, as well as value and energy, are embodied in our objective institutional classifications. As a special favor, will not the objective idealist show how, in some one single instance, his immanent " reason " makes any difference as respects the detection and elimination of error, or gives even the slightest assistance in discovering and validating the truly worthful? This practical work, the life blood of intelligence in everyday life and in critical science, is done by the despised and rejected matter of concrete empirical contexts and functions. Generalizing the issue: If the immanent organization be ascribed to thought, why should its work be such as to demand continuous correction and revision? If specific reflective thought, as empirical, be subject to all the limitations supposed to inhere in experience as such, how can it assume the burden of making good, of supplementing, reconstructing, and developing meanings? The logic of the case seems to be that Neo-Kantian idealism gets its status against empiricism by first accepting the Humian idea of experience, while the express import of its positive contribution is to show the *non-existence* (not merely the cognitive invalidity) of anything describable as mere states of subjective consciousness. Thus in the end it tends to destroy itself and to make way for a more adequate empiricism.

III

In the above discussion, I have unavoidably anticipated the second problem: the relation of conceptual thought to perceptual data. A distinct aspect still remains, however. Perception, as well as apriority, is a term harboring a fundamental ambiguity. It may mean (1) a distinct type of activity, predominantly practical in character, though carrying at its heart important cognitive and esthetic qualities; or (2) a distinctively cognitional experience, the function of observation as explicitly logical—a factor in science *qua* science.

In the first sense, as recent functional empiricism (working in harmony with psychology, but not itself peculiarly psychological) has abundantly shown, perception is primarily an act of adjustment of organism and environment, differing from a mere reflex or instinctive adaptation in that, in order to compensate for the failure of the instinctive adjustment, it requires an objective or discriminative presentation of conditions of action: the negative conditions or obstacles, and the positive conditions or means and resources.[1] This, of

---

[1] Compare, for example, Dr. Stuart's paper in the "Studies in Logical Theory," pp. 253-256. I may here remark that I remain totally unable to see how the *interpretation* of objectivity to mean controlling conditions of action (negative and positive as above) derogates at all from its naïve

course, is its cognitive phase. In so far as the material thus presented not only serves as a direct cue to further successful activity (successful in the overcoming of obstacles to the maintenance of the function entered upon) but presents auxiliary collateral objects and qualities that give additional range and depth of meaning to the activity of adjustment, perceiving is esthetic as well as intellectual.[1]

Now such perception cannot be made antithetical to thought, for it may itself be surcharged with any amount of imaginatively supplied and reflectively sustained ideal factors—such as are needed to determine and select relevant stimuli and to suggest and develop an appropriate plan and course of behavior. The amount of such saturating intellectual material depends upon the complexity and maturity of the behaving agent. Such perception, moreover, is strictly teleological, since it arises from an experienced need and functions to fulfil the purpose indicated by this need. The cognitional content is, indeed, carried by affectional and intentional contexts.

objectivity, or how it connotes cognitive subjectivity, or is in any way incompatible with a common-sense realistic theory of perception.

[1] For this suggested interpretation of the esthetic as surprising, or unintended, gratuitous collateral reinforcement, see Gordon, " Psychology of Meaning."

Then we have perception as scientific observation. This involves the deliberate, artful exclusion of affectional and purposive factors as exercising mayhap a vitiating influence upon the cognitive or objective content; or, more strictly speaking, a transformation of the more ordinary or "natural" emotional and purposive concomitants, into what Bain calls "neutral" emotion, and a purpose of finding out what the present conditions of the problem are. (The practical feature is not thus denied or eliminated, but the overweening influence of a present dominating end is avoided, so that *change of the character of the end* may be effected, if found desirable.) Here observation may be opposed to thought, in the sense that exact and minute description may be set over against interpretation, explanation, theorizing, and inference. In the wider sense of thought as equaling reflective process, the work of observation and description forms a constituent division of labor *within* thought. The impersonal demarcation and accurate registration of what is objectively there or present occurs for the sake (*a*) of eliminating meaning which is habitually but uncritically referred, and (*b*) of getting a basis for a meaning (at first purely inferential or hypothetical) that may be consistently referred; and that (*c*), resting upon examination and not upon mere *a priori* custom, may weather the strain of subsequent ex-

periences.   But in so far as thought is identified
with the conceptual phase as such of the entire
logical function, observation is, of course, set over
against thought: deliberately, purposely, and artfully so.

It is not uncommon to hear it said that the
Lockeian movement was all well enough for psychology, but went astray because it invaded the
field of logic.   If we mean by psychology a natural history of what at any time *passes* for knowledge, and by logic conscious control in the direction of grounded assurance, this remark appears
to reverse the truth.   As a natural history of
knowledge in the sense of opinion and belief,
Locke's account of discrete, simple ideas or meanings, which are compounded and then distributed,
does palpable violence to the facts.   But every
line of Locke shows that he was interested in knowledge in its honorific sense—controlled certainty,
or, where this is not feasible, measured probability.
And to logic as an account of the way in which
we by art build up a *tested* assurance, a rational-
ized conviction, Locke makes an important positive
contribution.   The pity is that he inclined to
take it for the whole of the logic of science,[1] not
seeing that it was but a correlative division of

---

[1] This, however, is not strictly true, since Locke goes far to
supply the means of his own correction in his account of the
" workmanship of the understanding."

labor to the work of hypotheses or inference; and that he tended to identify it with a natural history or psychology. The latter tendency exposed Locke to the Humian interpretation, and permanently sidetracked the positive contribution of his theory to logic, while it led to that confusion of an untrue psychology with a logic valid within limits, of which Mill is the standard example.

In analytic observation, it is a positive object to strip off all inferential meaning so far as may be—to reduce the facts as nearly as may be to derationalized data, in order to make possible a new and better rationalization. In and because of this process, the perceptual data approach the limit of a disconnected manifold, of the brutely given, of the merely sensibly present; while meaning stands out as a searched for principle of unification and explanation, that is, as a thought, a concept, an hypothesis. The extent to which this is carried depends wholly upon the character of the specific situation and problem; but, speaking generally, or of limiting tendencies, one may say it is carried to mere observation, pure brute description, on the one side, and to mere thought, that is hypothetical inference, on the other.

So far as Locke ignored this instrumental character of observation, he naturally evoked and strengthened rationalistic idealism; he called forth its assertion of the need of reason, of concepts, of universals, to constitute knowledge in its eulogistic sense. But two contrary errors do not make a truth, although they suggest and determine the nature of some relevant truth. This truth is the empirical origin, in a determinate type of situation, of the contrast of observation and conception; the empirical relevancy and the empirical worth of this contrast in controlling the character of subsequent experiences. To suppose that perception as it concretely exists, either in the early experiences of the animal, the race, or the individual, or in its later refined and expanded experiences, is identical with the sharply analyzed, objectively discriminated and internally disintegrated elements of scientific observation, is a perversion of experience; a perversion for which, indeed, professed empiricists set the example, but which idealism must perpetuate if it is not to find its end in an improved, functional empiricism.[1]

IV

We come now to the consideration of the third element in our problem; ideality, important and

---

[1] Plato, especially in his "Theætetus," seems to have begun the procedure of blasting the good name of perceptive experience by identifying a late and instrumental distinction, having to do with logical control, with all experience whatsoever.

normative value, in relation to experience; the antithesis of experience as a tentative, fragmentary, and ineffectual embodiment of meaning over against the perfect, eternal system of meanings which experience suggests even in nullifying and mutilating.

That from the *memory* standpoint experience presents itself as a multiplicity of episodic events with just enough continuity among them to suggest principles true " on the whole " or usually, but without furnishing instruction as to their exact range and bearing, seems obvious enough. Why should it not? The motive which leads to reflection on *past* experience could be satisfied in no other way. Continuities, connecting links, dynamic transitions drop out because, for the purpose of the recollection, they would be hindrances if now repeated; or because they are now available only when themselves objectified in definite terms and thus given a *quasi* independent, a *quasi* atomistic standing of their own. This is the only alternative to what the psychologists term " total reminiscence," which, so far as total, leave us with an elephant on our hands. Unless we are going to have a wholesale revivification of the past, giving us just another embarrassing present experience, illusory because irrelevant, memory must work by retail—by summoning *distinct* cases, events, sequences, precedents. Dis-membering is a positively necessary part of re-membering. But the resulting *disjecta membra* are in no sense experience as it was or is; they are simply elements held apart, and yet tentatively implicated together, in present experience for the sake of its most favorable evolution; evolution in the direction of the most excellent meaning or value conceived. If the remembering is efficacious and pertinent, it reveals the possibilities of the present; that is to say, it clarifies the transitive, transforming character that belongs inherently to the present. The dismembering of the vital present into the disconnected past is correlative to an anticipation, an idealization of the future.

Moreover, the contingent character of the principle or rule that emerges from a survey of cases, instances, as distinct from a fixed or necessary character, secures just what is wanted in the exigency of a prospective idealization, or refinement of excellence. It is just this character that secures flexibility and variety of outlook, that makes possible a consideration of alternatives and an attempt to select and to execute the more worthy among them. The fixed or necessary law would mean a future like the past—a dead, an unidealized future. It is exasperating to imagine how completely different would have been Aristotle's valuation of " experience " with respect to its contingency, if he had but once employed the function of developing and perfecting value, instead of the function of knowing an unalterable object, as the standard by which to estimate and measure intelligence.

The one constant trait of experience from its crudest to its most mature forms is that its contents undergo change of meaning, and of meaning in the sense of excellence, value. Every experience is in-course,[1] in course of becoming worse or better as to its contents, or in course of conscious endeavor to sustain some satisfactory level of value against encroachment or lapse. In this effort, both precedent, the reduction of the present idealization, the anticipation of the possible, though doubtful, future, emerge. Without idealization, that is, without conception of the favorable issue that the present, defined in terms of precedents, may portend in its transition, the recollection of precedents, and the formulation of tentative rules is nonsense. But without the identification of the present in terms of elements suggested by the past, without recognition, the ideal,

---

[1] Compare James, " Continuous transition is one sort of conjunctive relation; and to be a radical empiricist means to hold fast to this conjunctive relation of all others, for this is the strategic point, the position through which, if a hole be made, all the corruptions of dialectics and all the metaphysical fictions pour into our philosophy."—*Journal of Philosophy, Psychology, and Scientific Methods,* Vol. I., p. 536.

the value projected as end, remains inert, helpless, sentimental, without means of realization. Resembling cases and anticipation, memory and idealization, are the corresponding terms in which a present experience has its transitive force analyzed into reciprocally pertinent means and ends.

That an experience will change in content and value is the one thing certain. *How* it will change is the one thing naturally uncertain. Hence the import of the art of reflection and invention. Control of the character of the change in the direction of the worthful is the common business of theory and practice. Here is the province of the episodic recollection of past history and of the idealized foresight of possibilities. The irrelevancy of an objective idealism lies in the fact that it totally ignores the position and function of ideality in sustained and serious endeavor. Were values automatically injected and kept in the world of experience by any force not reflected in human memories and projects, it would make no difference whether this force were a Spencerian environment or an Absolute Reason. Did purpose ride in a cosmic automobile toward a predestined goal, it would not cease to be physical and mechanical in quality because labeled Divine Idea, or Perfect Reason. The moral would be " let us eat, drink, and be merry," for to-morrow—or if not this to-morrow, then upon some to-morrow, unaffected by our empirical memories, reflections, inventions, and idealizations—the cosmic automobile arrives. Spirituality, ideality, meaning as purpose, would be the last things to present themselves if objective idealism were true. Values cannot be both ideal and given, and their " given " character is emphasized, not transformed, when they are called eternal and absolute. But natural values become ideal the moment their maintenance is dependent upon the intentional activities of an empirical agent. To suppose that values are ideal because they are so eternally given is the contradiction in which objective idealism has intrenched itself. Objective ontological teleology spells machinery. Reflective and volitional, experimental teleology alone spells ideality.[1] Objective, rationalistic idealism breaks upon the fact that it can have no intermediary between a brutally achieved embodiment of meaning (physical in character or else of that peculiar quasi-physical character which goes generally by the name of metaphysical) and a total opposition of the given and the ideal, connoting their mutual indifference and incapacity. An empiricism that acknowledges the transitive character of experience, and that acknowledges the possible control

[1] One of the not least of the many merits of Santayana's " Life of Reason " is the consistency and vigor with which is upheld the doctrine that significant idealism means idealization.

óf the character of the transition by means of intelligent effort, has abundant opportunity to celebrate in productive art, genial morals, and impartial inquiry the grace and the severity of the ideal.

THE POSTULATE OF IMMEDIATE
EMPIRICISM [1]

THE criticisms made upon that vital but still unformed movement variously termed radical empiricism, pragmatism, humanism, functionalism, according as one or another aspect of it is uppermost, have left me with a conviction that the *fundamental* difference is not so much in matters overtly discussed as in a presupposition that remains tacit: a presupposition as to what experience is and means. To do my little part in clearing up the confusion, I shall try to make my own presupposition explicit. The object of this paper is, then, to set forth what I understand to be the postulate and the criterion of *immediate empiricism.* [2]

[1] Reprinted, with very slight change, from the *Journal of Philosophy, Psychology, and Scientific Methods,* Vol. II., No. 15, July, 1905.

[2] All labels are, of course, obnoxious and misleading. I hope, however, the term will be taken by the reader in the sense in which it is forthwith explained, and not in some more usual and familiar sense. Empiricism, as herein used, is as antipodal to sensationalistic empiricism, as it is to transcendentalism, and for the same reason. Both of these systems fall back on something which is defined in non-

Immediate empiricism postulates that things—anything, everything, in the ordinary or non-technical use of the term " thing "—are what they are experienced as. Hence, if one wishes to describe anything truly, his task is to tell what it is experienced as being. If it is a horse that is to be described, or the *equus* that is to be defined, then must the horse-trader, or the jockey, or the timid family man who wants a " safe driver," or the zoologist or the paleontologist tell us what the horse is which is experienced. If these accounts turn out different in some respects, as well as congruous in others, this is no reason for assuming the content of one to be exclusively "real," and that of others to be " phenomenal "; for each account of what is experienced will manifest that it is the account *of* the horse-dealer, or *of* the zoologist, and hence will give the conditions requisite for understanding the differences as well as the agreements of the various accounts. And the principle varies not a whit if we bring in the psychologist's horse, the logician's horse, or the metaphysician's horse.

directly-experienced terms in order to justify that which is directly experienced. Hence I have criticised such empiricism (*Philosophical Review,* Vol. XI., No. 4, p. 364) as essentially absolutistic in character; and also (" Studies in Logical Theory," pp. 30, 58) as an attempt to build up experience in terms of certain methodological checks and cues of attaining *certainty.*

In each case, the nub of the question is, *what sort of experience* is denoted or indicated: a concrete and determinate experience, varying, when it varies, in specific real elements, and agreeing, when it agrees, in specific real elements, so that we have a contrast, not between *a* Reality, and various approximations to, or phenomenal representations of Reality, but between different reals of experience. And the reader is begged to bear in mind that from this standpoint, when " an experience " or " some sort of experience " is referred to, " some thing " or " some sort of thing " is always meant.

Now, this statement that things are what they are experienced to be is usually translated into the statement that things (or, ultimately, Reality, Being) *are* only and just what they are *known* to be or that things are, or Reality *is*, what it is for a conscious knower—whether the knower be conceived primarily as a perceiver or as a thinker being a further, and secondary, question. This is the root-paralogism of all idealisms, whether subjective or objective, psychological or epistemological. By our postulate, things are what they are experienced to be; and, unless knowing is the sole and only genuine mode of experiencing, it is fallacious to say that Reality is just and exclusively what it is or would be to an all-competent allknower; or even that it *is*, relatively and piecemeal, what it is to a finite and partial knower.   Or, put more positively, knowing is one mode of experiencing, and the primary philosophic demand (from the standpoint of immediatism) is to find out *what* sort of an experience knowing is—or, concretely how things are experienced when they are experienced *as* known things.[1]   By concretely is meant, obviously enough (among other things), such an account of the experience of things as known that will bring out the characteristic traits and distinctions they possess as things of a knowing experience, as compared with things experienced esthetically, or morally, or economically, or technologically.   To assume that, because from the *standpoint of the knowledge experience* things *are* what they are known to be, therefore, metaphysically, absolutely, without qualification, everything in its reality (as distinct from its " appearance," or phenomenal occurrence) is what a knower would find it to be, is, from the immediatist's standpoint, if not the root of all philosophic evil, at least one of its main roots.   For this leaves out

[1] I hope the reader will not therefore assume that from the empiricist's standpoint knowledge is of small worth or import.   On the contrary, from the empiricist's standpoint it has *all* the worth which it is concretely experienced as possessing—which is simply tremendous.   But the exact *nature* of this worth is a thing to be found out in describing what we mean by experiencing objects as known—the actual differences made or found in experience.

of account what the knowledge standpoint is itself *experienced as*.

I start and am flustered by a noise heard.   Empirically, that noise *is* fearsome; it *really* is, not merely phenomenally or subjectively so.   That *is* *what* it is experienced as being.   But, when I experience the noise as a *known* thing, I find it to be innocent of harm.   It is the tapping of a shade against the window, owing to movements of the wind.   The experience has changed; that is, the thing experienced has changed—not that an unreality has given place to a reality, nor that some transcendental (unexperienced) Reality has changed,[1] not that truth has changed, but just and only the concrete reality experienced has changed.   I now feel ashamed of my fright; and the noise as fearsome is changed to noise as a windcurtain fact, and hence practically indifferent to my welfare.   This is a change of experienced existence effected through the medium of cognition.

---

[1] Since the non-empiricist believes in things-in-themselves (which he may term " atoms," " sensations," transcendental unities, *a priori* concepts, *an* absolute experience, or whatever), and since he finds that the empiricist makes much of change (as he must, since change is continuously experienced) he assumes that the empiricist means *his own* non-empirical Realities are in continual flux, and he naturally shudders at having his divinities so violently treated.   But, once recognize that the empiricist doesn't have any such Realities at all, and the entire problem of the relation of change to reality takes a very different aspect.

The content of the latter experience cognitively regarded is doubtless *truer* than the content of the earlier; but it is in no sense more real. To call it truer, moreover, must, from the empirical standpoint, mean a concrete *difference* in actual things experienced.[1] Again, in many cases, only in retrospect is the prior experience cognitionally regarded at all. In such cases, it is only in regard to contrasted content *in* a subsequent experience that the determination " truer " has force.

Perhaps some reader may now object that as matter of fact the entire experience *is* cognitive, but that the earlier parts of it are only imperfectly so, resulting in a phenomenon that is not real; while the latter part, being a more complete cognition, results in what is relatively, at least, more real.[2] In short, a critic may say that, when I was

---

[1] It would lead us aside from the point to try to tell just what is the nature of the experienced difference we call truth. Professor James's recent articles may well be consulted. The point to bear in mind here is just what sort of a thing the empiricist must mean by true, or truer (the noun Truth is, of course, a generic name for all cases of " Trues "). The adequacy of any particular account is not a matter to be settled by general reasoning, but by finding out what sort of an experience the truth-experience actually is.

[2] I say " relatively," because the transcendentalist still holds that finally the cognition is imperfect, giving us only some symbol or phenomenon of Reality (which *is* only in the Absolute or in some Thing-in-Itself)—otherwise the

frightened by the noise, I *knew* I was frightened; otherwise there would have been no experience at all.   At this point, it is necessary to make a distinction so simple and yet so all-fundamental that I am afraid the reader will be inclined to pooh-pooh it away as a mere verbal distinction.   But to see that to the empiricist this distinction is not verbal, but genuine, is the precondition of any understanding of him.   The immediatist must, by his postulate, ask what is the fright experienced *as*. Is what is actually experienced, I-know-I-am-frightened, or I-*am*-frightened?   I see absolutely no reason for claiming that the experience *must* be described by the former phrase.   In all probability (and all the empiricist logically needs is just one case of this sort) the experience is simply and just of fright-at-the-noise.   Later one may (or may not) have an experience describable *as* I-know-I-am- (or-was) and improperly or properly, frightened.   But this is a different experience— that is, a different *thing*.   And if the critic goes on to urge that the person " *really* " must have known that he was frightened, I can only point out that the critic is shifting the venue.   He may be right, but, if so, it is only because the " really "

curtain-wind fact would have as much ontological reality as the existence of the Absolute itself: a conclusion at which the non-empiricist perhorresces, for no reason obvious to me—save that it would put an end to his transcendentalism.

is something not concretely experienced (whose nature accordingly is the critic's business); and this is to depart from the empiricist's point of view, to attribute to him a postulate he expressly repudiates.

The material point may come out more clearly if I say that we must make a distinction between a thing as *cognitive*, and one as *cognized*.[1] I should define a cognitive experience as one that has certain bearings or implications which induce, and fulfil themselves in, a subsequent experience in which the relevant thing is experienced *as* cognized, *as* a known object, and is thereby transformed, or reorganized. The fright-at-the-noise in the case cited is obviously *cognitive*, in this sense. By description, it induces an investigation or inquiry in which both noise and fright are objectively stated or presented—the noise as a shade-wind fact, the fright as an organic reaction to a sudden acoustic stimulus, a reaction that under the given circumstances was useless or even detrimental, a maladaptation. Now, pretty much all of experience is of this sort (the " is " meaning, of course, is experienced *as*), and the empiricist is false to his principle if he does not duly note this fact.[2] But

---

[1] In general, I think the distinction between *-ive* and *-ed* one of the most fundamental of philosophic distinctions, and one of the most neglected. The same holds of *-tion* and *-ing*.

[2] What is criticised, now as "geneticism" (if I may coin

he is equally false to his principle if he permits himself to be confused as to the concrete differences in the two things experienced.

There are two little words through explication of which the empiricist's position may be brought out—" *as* " and " *that*." We may express his presupposition by saying that things are what they are experienced *as* being; or that to give a just account of anything is to tell what *that* thing is experienced to be. By these words I want to indicate the absolute, final, irreducible, and inexpugnable concrete *quale* which everything experienced not so much *has* as *is*. To grasp this aspect of empiricism is to see what the empiricist means by objectivity, by the element of control. Suppose we take, as a crucial case for the empiricist, an out and out illusion, say of Zöllner's lines. These are experienced as convergent; they are " truly " parallel. If things are what they are experienced as being, how can the distinction be drawn between illusion and the true state of the case? There is no answer to this question except by sticking to the fact that the experience of the lines as divergent is a concrete qualitative thing or *that*. It is *that* experience which it is, and no

the word) and now as " pragmatism " is, in its truth, just the fact that the empiricist does take account of the experienced " drift, occasion, and contexture " of things experienced—to use Hobbes's phrase.

other. And if the reader rebels at the iteration of such obvious tautology, I can only reiterate that the realization of the *meaning* of this tautology is the key to the whole question of the objectivity of experience, as that stands to the empiricist. The lines of *that* experience *are* divergent; not merely *seem* so. The question of truth is not as to whether Being or Non-Being, Reality or mere Appearance, is experienced, but as to the *worth* of a certain concretely experienced thing. The only way of passing upon this question is by sticking in the most uncompromising fashion to *that* experience as real. *That* experience is that two lines with certain cross-hatchings are apprehended as convergent; only by taking that experience as real and as fully real, is there any basis for, or way of going to, an experienced knowledge that the lines are parallel. It is in the concrete thing *as experienced* that all the grounds and clues to its own intellectual or logical rectification are contained. It is because this thing, afterwards adjudged false, is a concrete *that*, that it develops into a corrected experience (that is, experience of a corrected thing—we reform things just as we reform ourselves or a bad boy) whose full content is not a whit more real, but which is true or truer.[1]

[1] Perhaps the point would be clearer if expressed in this way: Except as subsequent estimates of *worth* are introduced, "real" means only existent. The eulogistic connota-

If *any* experience, then a *determinate* experience; and this determinateness is the only, and is the adequate, principle of control, or "objectivity." The experience may be of the vaguest sort. I may not see anything which I can identify as a familiar object—a table, a chair, etc. It may be dark; I may have only the vaguest impression that there is something which looks like a table. Or I may be completely befogged and confused, as when one rises quickly from sleep in a pitch-dark room. But this vagueness, this doubtfulness, this confusion is the thing experienced, and, *qua* real, is as " good " a reality as the self-luminous vision of an Absolute. It is not just vagueness, doubtfulness, confusion, at large or in general. It is *this* vagueness, and no other; absolutely unique, absolutely what *it* is.[1] Whatever gain in clearness, in fullness, in trueness of content is experienced must grow out of some element in the experience of *this* experienced *as* what it is. To return to the illusion: If the experience of the lines as convergent is illusory, it is because of some elements in the

tion that makes the term Reality equivalent to *true* or *genuine* being has great pragmatic significance, but its confusion with reality as existence is the point aimed at in the above paragraph.

[1] One does not so easily escape medieval Realism as one thinks. Either every experienced thing has its own determinateness, its own unsubstitutable, unredeemable reality, or else " generals " *are* separate existences after all.

thing as experienced, not because of something defined in terms of externality to this particular experience.   If the illusoriness can be detected, it is
because the thing experienced is real, having within
its experienced reality elements whose *own mutual*
tension effects its reconstruction.   Taken concretely, the experience of convergent lines con-
tains within itself the elements of the transformation of its own content.   It is *this* thing, and not
some separate truth, that clamors for its own
reform.   There is, then, from the empiricist's point
of view, no need to search for some aboriginal *that*
to which all successive experiences are attached,
and which is somehow thereby undergoing continuous change.   Experience is always of *thats*; and
the most comprehensive and inclusive experience
of the universe that the philosopher himself can
obtain is the experience of a characteristic *that*.
From the empiricist's point of view, this is as true
of the exhaustive and complete insight of a hypothetical all-knower as of the vague, blind experience of the awakened sleeper.   As reals, they stand
on the same level.   As trues, the latter has by
definition the better of it; but if this insight is in
any way the truth of the blind awakening, it is
because the latter has, in its *own* determinate *quale*,
elements of real continuity with the former; it is,
ex hypothesi, transformable through a series of
experienced reals without break of continuity, into

the absolute thought-experience.   There is no need
of logical manipulation to effect the transformation, nor *could* any logical consideration effect it.
If effected at all it is just by immediate experiences,
each of which is just as real (no more, no less)
as either of the two terms between which they lie.
Such, at least, is the meaning of the empiricist's
contention.   So, when he talks of experience, he
does not mean some grandiose, remote affair that
is cast like a net around a succession of fleeting
experiences; he does not mean an indefinite total,
comprehensive experience which somehow engirdles
an endless flux; he means that *things* are what
they are experienced to be, and that every experience is *some* thing.

From the postulate of empiricism, then (or, what
is the same thing, from a *general* consideration of
the concept of experience), nothing can be deduced,
not a single philosophical proposition.[1]   The reader

[1] Excepting, of course, some negative ones.   One could
say that certain views are certainly *not* true, because, by
hypothesis, they refer to nonentities, *i.e.*, non-empiricals.
But even here the empiricist must go slowly.   From his
own standpoint, even the most professedly transcendental
statements are, after all, real as experiences, and hence
negotiate some transaction with facts.   For this reason, he
cannot, in theory, reject them *in toto*, but has to show concretely how they arose and how they are to be corrected.
In a word, his logical relationship to statements that profess to relate to things-in-themselves, unknowables, inexperienced substances, etc., is precisely that of the psychologist
to the Zöllner lines.

may hence conclude that all this just comes to the truism that experience is experience, or is what it is. If one attempts to draw conclusions from the bare concept of experience, the reader is quite right. But the real significance of the principle is that of a method of philosophical analysis—a method identical in kind (but differing in problem and hence in operation) with that of the scientist. If you wish to find out what subjective, objective, physical, mental, cosmic, psychic, cause, substance, purpose, activity, evil, being, quality—any philosophic term, in short—means, go to experience and see what the thing is experienced *as*.

Such a method is not spectacular; it permits of no offhand demonstrations of God, freedom, immortality, nor of the exclusive reality of matter, or ideas, or consciousness, etc. But it supplies a way of telling what all these terms mean. It may seem insignificant, or chillingly disappointing, but only upon condition that it be not worked. Philosophic conceptions have, I believe, outlived their usefulness considered as stimulants to emotion, or as a species of sanctions; and a larger, more fruitful and more valuable career awaits them considered as specifically experienced meanings.

[NOTE: The reception of this essay proved that I was unreasonably sanguine in thinking that the foot-note of warning, appended to the title, would forfend radical misapprehension. I see now that it was unreasonable to expect that the word "immediate" in a philosophic writing could be generally understood to apply to anything except *knowl-edge,* even though the body of the essay is a protest against such limitation. But I venture to repeat that the essay is not a denial of the necessity of "mediation," or reflection, in knowledge, but is an assertion that the inferential factor must *exist,* or must occur, and that all existence is direct and vital, so that philosophy can pass upon its nature —as upon the nature of all of the rest of its subject-matter —only by first ascertaining what it exists or occurs *as.*

I venture to repeat also another statement of the text: I do not mean by "immediate experience" any aboriginal stuff out of which things are evolved, but I use the term to indicate the necessity of employing in philosophy the direct descriptive method that has now made its way in all the natural sciences, with such modifications, of course, as the subject itself entails.

There is nothing in the text to imply that things exist in experience atomically or in isolation. When it is said that a thing as cognized is *different* from an earlier non-cognitionally experienced thing, the saying no more implies lack of continuity between the things, than the obvious remark that a seed is different from a flower or a leaf denies their continuity. The amount and kind of continuity or discreteness that exists is to be discovered by recurring to what actually occurs in experience.

Finally, there is nothing in the text that denies the existence of things temporally prior to human experiencing of them. Indeed, I should think it fairly obvious that we experience most things *as* temporally prior to our experiencing of them. The import of the article is to the effect that we are not entitled to draw philosophic (as distinct from scientific) conclusions as to the meaning of prior temporal existence till we have ascertained what it is to experience a thing as past. These four disclaimers cover, I think, all the misapprehensions disclosed in the four or five controversial articles (noted below) that the original essay evoked. One of these articles (that of Professor

Woodbridge), raised a point of fact, holding that cognitional experience tells us, without alteration, just what the things of other types of experience are, and in that sense transcends other experiences. This is too fundamental an issue to discuss in a note, and I content myself with remarking that with respect to it, the bearing of the article is that the issue must be settled by a careful descriptive survey of things as experienced, to see whether modifications do not occur in existences when they are experienced *as* known; *i.e.*, as true or false in character. The reader interested in following up this discussion is referred to the following articles: Vol. II. of the *Journal of Philosophy, Psychology, and Scientific Methods,* two articles by Bakewell, p. 520 and p. 687; one by Bode, p. 658; one by Woodbridge, p. 573; Vol. III. of the same Journal, by Leighton, p. 174.]

"CONSCIOUSNESS" AND EXPERIENCE [1]

EVERY science in its final standpoint and working aims is controlled by conditions lying outside itself—conditions that subsist in the practical life of the time. With no science is this as obviously true as with psychology. Taken without nicety of analysis, no one would deny that psychology is specially occupied with the individual; that it wishes to find out those things that proceed peculiarly from the individual, and the mode of their connection with him. Now, the way in which the individual is conceived, the value that is attributed to him, the things in his make-up that arouse interest, are not due at the outset to psychology. The scientific view regards these matters in a reflected, a borrowed, medium. They are revealed in the light of social life. An autocratic, an aristocratic, a democratic society propound such different estimates of the worth and place of individuality; they procure for the individual as an individual such different sorts of experience;

[1] Delivered as a public address before the Philosophic Union of the University of California, with the title "Psychology and Philosophic Method," May, 1899, and published in the *University Chronicle* for August, 1899. Reprinted, with slight verbal changes, mostly excisions.

they aim at arousing such different impulses and at organizing them according to such different purposes, that the psychology arising in each must show a different temper.

In this sense, psychology is a political science. While the professed psychologist, in his conscious procedure, may easily cut his subject-matter loose from these practical ties and references, yet the starting point and goal of his course are none the less socially set. In this conviction I venture to introduce to an audience that could hardly be expected to be interested in the technique of psychology, a technical subject, hoping that the human meaning may yet appear.

There is at present a strong, apparently a growing tendency to conceive of psychology as an account of the consciousness of the individual, considered as something in and by itself; consciousness, the assumption virtually runs, being of such an order that it may be analyzed, described, and explained in terms of just itself. The statement, as commonly made, is that psychology is an account of consciousness, *qua* consciousness; and the phrase is supposed to limit psychology to a certain definite sphere of fact that may receive adequate discussion for scientific purposes, without troubling itself with what lies outside. Now if this conception be true, there is no intimate, no important connection of psychology and philosophy at large.

That philosophy, whose range is comprehensive, whose problems are catholic, should be held down by a discipline whose voice is as partial as its material is limited, is out of the range of intelligent discussion.

But there is another possibility. If the individual of whom psychology treats be, after all, a social individual, any absolute setting off and apart of a sphere of consciousness as, even for scientific purposes, self-sufficient, is condemned in advance. All such limitation, and all inquiries, descriptions, explanations that go with it, are only preliminary. "Consciousness" is but a symbol, an anatomy whose life is in natural and social operations. To know the symbol, the psychical letter, is important; but its necessity lies not within itself, but in the need of a language for reading the things signified. If this view be correct, we cannot be so sure that psychology is without large philosophic significance. Whatever meaning the individual has for the social life that he both incorporates and animates, that meaning has psychology for philosophy.

This problem is too important and too large to suffer attack in an evening's address. Yet I venture to consider a portion of it, hoping that such things as appear will be useful clues in entering wider territory. We may ask what is the effect upon psychology of considering its material as something so distinct as to be capable of treatment without involving larger issues. In this inquiry we take as representative some such account of the science as this: Psychology deals with consciousness " as such " in its various modes and processes. It aims at an isolation of each such as will permit accurate description: at statement of its place in the serial order such as will enable us to state the laws by which one calls another into being, or as will give the natural history of its origin, maturing, and dissolution. It is both analytic and synthetic—analytic in that it resolves each state into its constituent elements; synthetic in that it discovers the processes by which these elements combine into complex wholes and series. It leaves alone—it shuts out—questions concerning the validity, the objective import of these modifications: of their value in conveying truth, in effecting goodness, in constituting beauty. For it is just with such questions of worth, of validity, that philosophy has to do.

Some such view as this is held by the great majority of working psychologists to-day. A variety of reasons have conspired to bring about general acceptance. Such a view seems to enroll one in the ranks of the scientific men rather than of the metaphysicians—and there are those who distrust the metaphysicians. Others desire to take problems piecemeal and in detail, avoiding that excursion into ultimates, into that never-ending panorama of new questions and new possibilities that seems to be the fate of the philosopher. While no temperate mind can do other than sympathize with this view, it is hardly more than an expedient. For, as Mr. James remarks, after disposing of the question of free-will by relegating it to the domain of the metaphysician:—" Metaphysics means only an unusually obstinate attempt to think clearly and consistently "—and clearness and consistency are not things to be put off beyond a certain point. When the metaphysician chimes in with this new-found modesty of the psychologist, so different from the disposition of Locke and Hume and the Mills, salving his metaphysical conscience with the remark—it hardly possesses the dignity of a conviction—that the partial sciences, just because they are partial, are not expected to be coherent with themselves nor with one another; when the metaphysician, I say, praises the psychologist for sticking to his last, we are reminded that another motive is also at work. There is a half-conscious irony in this abnegation of psychology. It is not the first time that science has assumed the work of Cinderella; and, since Mr. Huxley has happily reminded her, she is not altogether oblivious, in her modesty, of a possible future check to the pride of her haughty sister, and of a certain coronation that shall mark her coming to her own.

But, be the reasons as they may, there is little doubt of the fact. Almost all our working psychologists admit, nay, herald this limitation of their work. I am not presumptuous enough to set myself against this array. I too proclaim myself of those who believe that psychology has to do (at a certain point, that is) with " consciousness as such." But I do not believe that the limitation is final. Quite the contrary: if " consciousness " or " state of consciousness " be given intelligible meaning, I believe that this conception is the open gateway into the fair fields of philosophy. For, note you, the phrase is an ambiguous one. It may mean one thing to the metaphysician who proclaims: Here finally we have psychology recognizing her due metes and bounds, giving bonds to trespass no more. It may mean quite another thing to the psychologist in his work—whatever he may happen to say about it. It may be that the psychologist deals with states of consciousness as the significant, the analyzable and describable form, to which he reduces the things he is studying. Not that they *are* that existence, but that they are its indications, its clues, in shape for handling by scientific methods. So, for example, does the paleontologist work. Those curiously shaped and marked forms to which he is devoted are not life, nor are they the literal termini of his endeavor; but through them as signs and records

he construes a life.   And again, the painter-artist
might well say that he is concerned only with
colored paints as such.   Yet none the less through
them as registers and indices, he reveals to us
the mysteries of sunny meadow, shady forest, and
twilight wave.   These are the things-in-themselves
of which the oils on his palette are phenomena.

So the preoccupation of the psychologist with
states of consciousness may signify that they are
the media, the concrete conditions to which he
purposely reduces his material, in order, *through
them*, as methodological helps, to get at and understand that which is anything but a state of consciousness.   To him, however, who insists upon the
fixed and final limitation of psychology, the state
of consciousness is not the shape some fact takes
from the exigency of investigation; it is literally
the full fact itself.   It is not an intervening term;
it bounds the horizon.   Here, then, the issue defines itself.   I conceive that states of consciousness (and I hope you will take the phrase broadly
enough to cover all the specific data of psychology) have no existence before the psychologist
begins to work.   He brings them into existence.
What we are really after is the process of experience, the way in which it arises and behaves.
We want to know its course, its history, its laws.
We want to know its various typical forms; how
each originates; how it is related to others; the

part it plays in maintaining an inclusive, expanding, connected course of experience. Our problem as psychologists is to learn its *modus operandi*, its method.

The paleontologist is again summoned to our aid. In a given district he finds a great number and variety of footprints. From these he goes to work to construct the structure and the life habits of the animals that made them. The tracks exist undoubtedly; they are there; but yet he deals with them not as final existences but as signs, phenomena in the literal sense. Imagine the hearing that the critic would receive who should inform the paleontologist that he is transcending his field of scientific activity; that his concern is with footprints as such, aiming to describe each, to analyze it into its simplest forms, to compare the different kinds with one another so as to detect common elements, and finally, thereby, to discover the laws of their arrangement in space!

Yet the immediate data are footprints, and footprints only. The paleontologist does in a way do all these things that our imaginary critic is urging upon him. The difference is not that he arbitrarily lugs in other data; that he invents entities and faculties that are not there. The difference is in his standpoint. His interest is in the animals, and the data are treated in whatever way seems likely to serve this interest. So with the psychologist. He is continually and perforce occupied with minute and empirical investigation of special facts—states of consciousness, if you please. But these neither define nor exhaust his scientific problem. They are his footprints, his clues through which he places before himself the life-process he is studying—with the further difference that his footprints are not after all given to him, but are developed by his investigation.[1]

The supposition that these states are somehow existent by themselves and in this existence provide the psychologist with ready-made material is just the supreme case of the " psychological fallacy ": the confusion of experience as it is to the one experiencing with what the psychologist makes out of it with his reflective analysis.

The psychologist begins with certain operations, acts, functions as his data. If these fall out of

---

[1] This is a fact not without its bearings upon the question of the nature and value of introspection. The objection that introspection "alters" the reality and hence is untrustworthy, most writers dispose of by saying that, after all, it need not alter the reality so very much—not beyond repair— and that, moreover, memory assists in restoring the ruins. It would be simpler to admit the fact: that the purpose of introspection is precisely to effect the right sort of alteration. If introspection should give us the original experience again, we should just be living through the experience over again in direct fashion; as psychologists we should not be forwarded one bit. Reflection upon this obvious proposition may bring to light various other matters worthy of note.

sight in the course of discussion, it is only because having been taken for granted, they remain to control the whole development of the inquiry, and to afford the sterling medium of redemption. Acts such as perceiving, remembering, intending, loving give the points of departure; they alone are concrete experiences. To understand these experiences, under what conditions they arise, and what effects they produce, analysis into states of consciousness occurs. And the modes of consciousness that are figured remain unarranged and unimportant, save as they may be translated back into acts.

To remember is to do something, as much as to shoe a horse, or to cherish a keepsake. To propose, to observe, to be kindly affectioned, are terms of value, of practice, of operation; just as digestion, respiration, locomotion express functions, not observable " objects." But there is an object that may be described: lungs, stomach, leg-muscles, or whatever. Through the structure we present to ourselves the function; it appears laid out before us, spread forth in detail—objectified in a word. The anatomist who devotes himself to this detail may, if he please (and he probably does please to concentrate his devotion) ignore the function: to discover what is there, to analyze, to measure, to describe, gives him outlet enough. But nevertheless it is the function that fixed the point of departure, that prescribed the problem and that set the limits, physical as well as intellectual, of subsequent investigation. Reference to function makes the details discovered other than a jumble of incoherent trivialities. One might as well devote himself to the minute description of a square yard of desert soil were it not for this translation. States of consciousness are the morphology of certain functions.[1] What is true of analysis, of description, is true equally of classification. Knowing, willing, feeling, name states of consciousness not in terms of themselves, but in terms of acts, attitudes, found in experience.[2]

---

[1] Thus to divorce " structure psychology " from " function psychology " is to leave us without possibility of scientific comprehension of function, while it deprives us of all standard of reference in selecting, observing, and explaining the structure.

[2] The following answer may fairly be anticipated: " This is true of the operations cited, but only because complex processes have been selected. Such a term as ' knowing ' does of course express a function involving a system of intricate references. But, for that very reason, we go back to the sensation which is the genuine type of the ' state of consciousness ' as such, pure and unadulterate and unsophisticated." The point is large for a footnote, but the following considerations are instructive: (1) The same psychologist will go on to inform us that sensations, as we experience them, are networks of reference—they are perceptual, and more or less conceptual even. From which it would appear that whatever else they are or are not, the sensations, for which self-inclosed existence is claimed, are *not* states of consciousness. And (2) we are told that

Explanation, even of an " empirical sort " is as impossible as determination of a " state " and its classification, when we rigidly confine ourselves to modifications of consciousness as a self-existent. Sensations are always defined, classified, and explained by reference to conditions which, according to the theory, are extraneous—sense-organs and stimuli. The whole physiological side assumes a ludicrously anomalous aspect on this basis.[1] While experimentation is retained, and even made much of, it is at the cost of logical coherence. To experiment with reference to a bare state of consciousness is a performance of which one cannot imagine the nature, to say nothing of doing it; while to experiment with reference to acts and the conditions of their occurrence is a natural and straightforward undertaking. Such simple processes as association are concretely inexplicable when

these are reached by scientific abstraction in order to account for complex forms. From which it would appear that they are hypothecated as products of interpretation and for purposes of further interpretation. Only the delusion that the more complex forms are just aggregates (instead of being acts, like seeing, hoping, etc.) prevents recognition of the point in question—that the "state of consciousness" is an instrument of inquiry or methodological appliance.

[1] On the other hand, if what we are trying to get at is just the course and procedure of experiencing, of course any consideration that helps distinguish and make comprehensible that process is thoroughly pertinent.

we assume states of consciousness as existences by themselves. As recent psychology testifies, we again have to resort to conditions that have no place nor calling on the basis of the theory—the principle of habit, of neural action, or else some connection in the object.[1]

We have only to note that there are two opposing schools in psychology to see in what an unscientific status is the subject. We have only to consider that these two schools are the result of assuming states of consciousness as existences *per se* to locate the source of the scientific scandal. No matter what the topic, whether memory or association or attention or effort, the same dualisms present themselves, the same necessity of choosing between two schools. One, lost in the distinctions that it has developed, denies the function because it can find objectively presented only states of consciousness. So it abrogates the function, regarding it as a mere aggregate of such states, or as a purely external and factitious re-

[1] It may avoid misunderstanding if I anticipate here a subsequent remark: that my point is not in the least that "states of consciousness" require some "synthetic unity" or faculty of substantial mind to effect their association. Quite the contrary; for this theory also admits the "states of consciousness" as existences in themselves also. My contention is that the "state of consciousness" as such is always a methodological product, developed in the course and for the purposes of psychological analysis.

lation between them. The other school, recognizing that this procedure explains away rather than explains, the values of experience, attempts to even up by declaring that certain functions are themselves immediately given data of consciousness, existing side by side with the " states," but indefinitely transcending them in worth, and apprehended by some higher organ. So against the elementary contents and external associations of the analytic school in psychology, we have the complicated machinery of the intellectualist school, with its pure self-consciousness as a source of ultimate truths, its hierarchy of intuitions, its ready-made faculties. To be sure, these " spiritual faculties " are now largely reduced to some one comprehensive form—Apperception, or Will, or Attention, or whatever the fashionable term may be. But the principle remains the same; the assumption of a function as a given existent, distinguishable in itself and acting upon other existences—as if the functions digestion and vision were regarded as separate from organic structures, somehow acting upon them from the outside so as to bring cooperation and harmony into them![1] This division into psychological schools is as reasonable as would be one of botanists into rootists and flowerists; of

---

[1] The " functions " are in truth ordinary everyday acts and attitudes: seeing, smelling, talking, listening, remembering, hoping, loving, fearing.

those proclaiming the root to be the rudimentary and essential structure, and those asserting that since the function of seed-bearing is the main thing, the flower is really the controlling "synthetic" principle.   Both sensationalist and intellectualist suppose that psychology has some special sphere of " reality " or of experience marked off for it within which the data are just lying around, self-existent and ready-made, to be picked up and assorted as pebbles await the visitor on the beach. Both alike fail to recognize that the psychologist first has experience to deal with; the same experience that the zoologist, geologist, chemist, mathematician, and historian deal with, and that what characterizes his specialty is not some data or existences which he may call uniquely his own; but the problem raised—the problem of the *course* of the acts that constitute experiencing.

Here psychology gets its revenge upon those who would rule it out of possession of important philosophical bearing.   As a matter of fact, the larger part of the questions that are being discussed in current epistemology and what is termed metaphysic of logic and ethic arise out of (and are hopelessly compromised by) this original assumption of " consciousness as such "—in other words, are provoked by the exact reason that is given for denying to psychology any essential meaning for epistemology and metaphysic.   Such is the

irony of the situation. The epistemologist's problem is, indeed, usually put as the question of how
the subject can so far " transcend " itself as to
get valid assurance of the objective world. The
very phraseology in which the problem is put reveals the thoroughness of the psychologist's revenge. Just and only because experience has been
reduced to " states of consciousness " as independent existences, does the question of self-transcend-
ence have any meaning. The entire epistemological industry is one—shall I say it—of a Sisyphean
nature. *Mutatis mutandis*, the same holds of the
metaphysic of logic, ethic, and esthetic. In each
case, the basic problem has come to be how a mere
state of consciousness can be the vehicle of a system
of truth, of an objectively valid good, of beauty
which is other than agreeable feeling. We may, indeed, excuse the psychologist for not carrying on
the special inquiries that are the business of logical, ethical, and esthetical philosophy; but can we
excuse ourselves for forcing his results into such
a shape as to make philosophic problems so arbitrary that they are soluble only by arbitrarily
wrenching scientific facts?

Undoubtedly we are between two fires. In plac-
ing upon psychology the responsibility of discovering the method of experience, as a sequence of
acts and passions, do we not destroy just that
limitation to concrete detail which now constitutes

it a science? Will not the psychologist be the first to repudiate this attempt to mix him up in matters philosophical? We need only to keep in mind the specific facts involved in the term Course or Process of Experience to avoid this danger. The immediate preoccupation of the psychologist is with very definite and empirical facts—questions like the limits of audition, of the origin of pitch, of the structure and conditions of the musical scale, etc. Just so the immediate affair of the geologist is with particular rock-structures, of the botanist with particular plants, and so on. But through the collection, description, location, classification of rocks the geologist is led to the splendid story of world-forming. The limited, fixed, and separate piece of work is dissolved away in the fluent and dynamic drama of the earth. So, the plant leads with inevitableness to the whole process of life and its evolution.

In form, the botanist still studies the genus, the species, the plant—hardly, indeed, that; rather the special parts, the structural elements, of the plant. In reality, he studies life itself; the structures are the indications, the signature through which he renders transparent the mystery of life growing in the changing world. It was doubtless necessary for the botanist to go through the Linnean period—the period of engagement with rigid detail and fixed classifications; of tear-

ing apart and piecing together; of throwing all
emphasis upon peculiarities of number, size, and
appearance of matured structure; of regarding
change, growth, and function as external, more or
less interesting, attachments to form. Examination of this period is instructive; there is much in
contemporary investigation and discussion that is
almost unpleasantly reminiscent in its suggestive-
ness. The psychologist should profit by the intervening history of science. The conception of evolution is not so much an additional law as it is a
face-about. The fixed structure, the separate
form, the isolated element, is henceforth at best a
mere stepping-stone to knowledge of process, and
when not at its best, marks the end of comprehension, and betokens failure to grasp the problem.

With the change in standpoint from self-in-
cluded existence to including process, from structural unit of composition to controlling unity of
function, from changeless form to movement in
growth, the whole scheme of values is transformed.
Faculties are definite directions of development;
elements are products that are starting-points for
new processes; bare facts are indices of change;
static conditions are modes of accomplished adjustment. Not that the concrete, empirical phenomenon loses in worth, much less that unverifiable
"metaphysical" entities are impertinently introduced; but that our aim is the discovery of a

process of actions in its adaptations to circumstance. If we apply this evolutionary logic in psychology, where shall we stop? Questions of limits of stimuli in a given sense, say hearing, are in reality questions of temporary arrests, adjustments marking the favorable equilibrium of the whole organism; they connect with the question of the use of sensation in general and auditory sensations in particular for life-habits; of the origin and use of localized and distinguished perception; and this, in turn, involves within itself the whole question of space and time recognition; the significance of the thing-and-quality experience, and so on. And when we are told that the question of the origin of space experience has nothing at all to do with the question of the nature and significance of the space experienced, the statement is simply evidence that the one who makes it is still at the static standpoint; he believes that things, that relations, have existence and significance apart from the particular conditions under which they come into experience, and apart from the special service rendered in those particular conditions.

Of course, I am far from saying that every psychologist must make the whole journey. Each individual may contract, as he pleases, for any section or subsection he prefers; and undoubtedly the well-being of the science is advanced by such division of labor. But psychology goes over the whole ground from detecting every distinct act of experiencing, to seeing what need calls out the special organ fitted to cope with the situation, and discovering the machinery through which it operates to keep a-going the course of action.

But, I shall be told, the wall that divides psychology from philosophy cannot be so easily treated as non-existent. Psychology is a matter of natural history, even though it may be admitted that it is the natural history of the course of experience. But philo:ophy is a matter of values; of the criticism and justification of certain validities. One deals, it is said, with genesis, with conditions of temporal origin and transition; the other with analysis, with eternal constitution. I shall have to repeat that just this rigid separation of genesis and analysis seems to me a survival from a pre-evolutionary, a pre-historic age. It indicates not so much an assured barrier between philosophy and psychology as the distance dividing philosophy from all science. For the lesson that mathematicians first learned, that physics and chemistry pondered over, in which the biological disciplines were finally tutored, is that sure and delicate analysis is possible only through the patient study of conditions of origin and development. The method of analysis in mathematics is the method of construction. The experimental method is the method of making, of following the history of production; the term " cause " that has (when taken as an existent entity) so hung on the heels of science as to impede its progress, has universal meaning when read as condition of appearance in a process. And, as already intimated, the conception of evolution is no more and no less the discovery of a general law of life than it is the generalization of all scientific method. Everywhere analysis that cannot proceed by examining the successive stages of its subject, from its beginning up to its culmination, that cannot control this examination by discovering the conditions under which successive stages appear, is only preliminary. It may further the invention of proper tools of inquiry, it may help define problems, it may serve to suggest valuable hypotheses. But as science it breathes an air already tainted. There is no way to sort out the results flowing from the subject-matter itself from those introduced by the assumptions and presumptions of our own reflection. Not so with natural history when it is worthy of its name. Here the analysis is the unfolding of the existence itself. Its distinctions are not pigeon-holes of our convenience; they are stakes that mark the parting of the ways in the process itself. Its classifications are not a grasp at factors resisting further analysis; they are the patient tracings of the paths pursued. Nothing is more out of date than to suppose that interest in genesis is interest in reducing higher forms to cruder ones: it is interest in locating the exact and objective conditions under which a given fact appears, and in relation to which accordingly it has its meaning. Nothing is more naïve than to suppose that in pursuing " natural history " (term of scorn in which yet resides the dignity of the world-drama) we simply learn something of the temporal conditions under which a given value appears, while its own eternal essential quality remains as opaque as before. Nature knows no such divorce of quality and circumstance. Things come when they are wanted and as they are wanted; their quality is precisely the response they give to the conditions that call for them, while the furtherance they afford to the movement of their whole is their meaning. The severance of analysis and genesis, instead of serving as a ready-made test by which to try out the empirical, temporal events of psychology from the rational abiding constitution of philosophy, is a brand of philosophic dualism: the supposition that values are externally obtruded and statically set in irrelevant rubbish.

There are those who will admit that " states of consciousness " are but the cross-sections of flow of behavior, arrested for inspection, made in order that we may reconstruct experience in its life-

history. Yet in the knowledge of the course and
method of our experience, they will hold that we
are far from the domain proper of philosophy.
Experience, they say, is just the historic achievement of finite individuals; it tells the tale of approach to the treasures of truth, of partial victory, but larger defeat, in laying hold of the
treasure. But, they say, reality is not the path
to reality, and record of devious wanderings in the
path is hardly a safe account of the goal. Psychology, in other words, may tell us something of how
we mortals lay hold of the world of things and
truths; of how we appropriate and assimilate its
contents; and of how we react. It may trace the
issues of such approaches and apprehensions upon
the course of our own individual destinies. But it
cannot wisely ignore nor sanely deny the distinction between these individual strivings and achievements, and the " Reality " that subsists and supports its own structure outside these finite futilities.
The processes by which we turn over The Reality
into terms of our fragmentary unconcluded, in-
conclusive experiences are so extrinsic to the Reality itself as to have no revealing power with reference to it. There is the *ordo ad universum*, the
subject of philosophy; there is the *ordo ad in-
dividuum*, the subject of psychology.

Some such assumption as this lies latent, I am
convinced, in all forswearings of the kinship of

psychology and philosophy. Two conceptions hang together. The opinion that psychology is an account only and finally of states of consciousness, and therefore can throw no light upon the objects with which philosophy deals, is twin to the doctrine that the whole conscious life of the individual is not organic to the world. The philosophic basis and scope of this doctrine lie beyond examination here. But even in passing one cannot avoid remarking that the doctrine is almost never consistently held; the doctrine logically carried out leads so directly to intellectual and moral scepticism that the theory usually prefers to work in the dark background as a disposition and temper of thought rather than to make a frank statement of itself. Even in the half-hearted expositions of the process of human experience as something merely annexed to the reality of the universe, we are brought face to face to the consideration with which we set out: the dependence of theories of the individual upon the position at a given time of the individual practical and social. The doctrine of the accidental, futile, transitory significance of the individual's experience as compared with eternal realities; the notion that at best the individual is simply realizing for and in himself what already has fixed completeness in itself is congruous only with a certain intellectual and political scheme and must modify itself as that shifts. When such re-

arrangement comes, our estimate of the nature
and importance of psychology will mirror the
change.

When man's command of the methods that control action was precarious and disturbed; when
the tools that subject the world of things and
forces to use and operation were rare and clumsy,
it was unavoidable that the individual should sub-
mit his perception and purpose blankly to the
blank reality beyond. Under such circumstances,
external authority must reign; the belief that human experience in itself is approximate, not intrinsic, is inevitable. Under such circumstances,
reference to the individual, to the subject, is a resort only for explaining error, illusion, and uncertainty. The necessity of external control and external redemption of experience reports itself in a
low valuation of the self, and of all the factors and
phases of experience that spring from the self.
That the psychology of medievalism should appear
only as a portion of its theology of sin and salvation is as obvious as that the psychology of the
Greeks should be a chapter of cosmology.

As against all this, the assertion is ventured
that psychology, supplying us with knowledge of
the behavior of experience, is a conception of democracy. Its postulate is that since experience
fulfils itself in individuals, since it administers
itself through their instrumentality, the account of

the course and method of this achievement is a significant and indispensable affair.

Democracy is possible only because of a change in intellectual conditions. It implies tools for getting at truth in detail, and day by day, as we go along. Only such possession justifies the surrender of fixed, all-embracing principles to which, as universals, all particulars and individuals are subject for valuation and regulation. Without such possession, it is only the courage of the fool that would undertake the venture to which democracy has committed itself—the ordering of life in response to the needs of the moment in accordance with the ascertained truth of the moment. Modern life involves the deification of the here and the now; of the specific, the particular, the unique, that which happens once and has no measure of value save such as it brings with itself. Such deification is monstrous fetishism, unless the deity be there; unless the universal lives, moves, and has its being in experience as individualized.[1] This con-

---

[1] This is perhaps a suitable moment to allude to the absence, in this discussion, of reference to what is sometimes termed rational psychology—the assumption of a separate, substantialized ego, soul, or whatever, existing side by side with particular experiences and "states of consciousness," acting upon them and acted upon by them. In ignoring this and confining myself to the "states of consciousness" theory and the "natural history" theory, I may appear not only to have unduly narrowed the concerns

viction of the value of the individualized finds its further expression in psychology, which undertakes to show how this individualization proceeds, and in what aspect it presents itself.

Of course, such a conception means something for philosophy as well as for psychology; possibly it involves for philosophy the larger measure of transformation. It involves surrender of any claim on the part of philosophy to be the sole source of some truths and the exclusive guardian of some

at issue, but to have weakened my own point, as this doctrine seems to offer a special vantage ground whence to defend the close relationship of psychology and philosophy. The "narrowing," if such it be, will have to pass—from limits of time and other matters. But the other point I cannot concede. The independently existing soul restricts and degrades individuality, making of it a separate thing outside of the full flow of things, alien to things experienced and consequently in either mechanical or miraculous relations to them. It is vitiated by just the quality already objected to—that psychology has a separate piece of reality apportioned to it, instead of occupying itself with the manifestation and operation of any and all existences in reference to concrete action. From this point of view, the "states of consciousness" attitude is a much more hopeful and fruitful one. It ignores certain considerations, to be sure; and when it turns its ignoring into denial, it leaves us with curious hieroglyphics. But after all, there is a key; these symbols can be read; they may be translated into terms of the course of experience. When thus translated, selfhood, individuality, is neither wiped out nor set up as a miraculous and foreign entity; it is seen as the unity of reference and function involved in all things when fully experienced—the pivot about which they turn.

values. It means that philosophy be a method; not an assurance company, nor a knight errant. It means an alignment with science. Philosophy may not be sacrificed to the partial and superficial clamor of that which sometimes officiously and pretentiously exhibits itself as Science. But there is a sense in which philosophy must go to school to the sciences; must have no data save such as it receives at their hands; and be hospitable to no method of inquiry or reflection not akin to those in daily use among the sciences. As long as it claims for itself special territory of fact, or peculiar modes of access to truth, so long must it occupy a dubious position. Yet this claim it has to make until psychology comes to its own. There is something in experience, something in things, which the physical and the biological sciences do not touch; something, moreover, which is not just more experiences or more existences; but without which their materials are inexperienced, unrealized. Such sciences deal only with what *might* be experienced; with the content of experience, provided and assumed there be experience. It is psychology which tells us how this possible experience loses its barely hypothetical character, and is stamped with categorical unquestioned experiencedness; how, in a word, it becomes here and now in some uniquely individualized life. Here is the necessary transition of science into philosophy; a passage that carries the verified and solid body of the one into the large and free form of the other.

[NOTE: I have let this paper stand much as written, though now conscious that much more is crowded into it than could properly be presented in one paper. The drift of the ten years from '99 to '09 has made, I venture to believe, for increased clearness in the main positions of the paper: The revival of a naturalistic realism, the denial of the existence of "consciousness," the development of functional and dynamic psychology (accompanied by aversion to interpretation of functions as faculties of a soul-substance)—all of these tendencies are sympathetic with the aim of the paper. There is another reason for letting it stand: the new functional and pragmatic empiricism proffered in this volume has been constantly objected to on the ground that its conceptions of knowledge and verification lead only to subjectivism and solipsism. The paper may indicate that the identification of experience with bare states of consciousness represents the standpoint of the critic, not of the empiricism criticised, and that it is for him, not for me, to fear the subjective implications of such a position. The paper also clearly raises the question as to how far the isolation of "consciousness" from nature and social life, which characterizes the procedure of many psychologists of to-day, is responsible for keeping alive quite unreal problems in philosophy.]

THE SIGNIFICANCE OF THE PROBLEM
OF KNOWLEDGE [1]

IT is now something over a century since Kant
called upon philosophers to cease their discussion regarding the nature of the world and the
principles of existence until they had arrived at
some conclusion regarding the nature of the knowing process. But students of philosophy know
that Kant formulated the question " how knowledge is possible " rather than created it. As matter of fact, reflective thought for two centuries
before Kant had been principally interested in just
this problem, although it had not generalized its
own interest. Kant brought to consciousness the
controlling motive. The discussion, both in Kant
himself and in his successors, often seems scholastic, lost in useless subtlety, scholastic argument,
and technical distinctions. Within the last decade
in particular there have been signs of a growing
weariness as to epistemology, and a tendency to

[1] Delivered before the Philosophical Club of the University of Michigan, in the winter of 1897, and reprinted with
slight change from a monograph in the " University of Chicago Contributions to Philosophy," 1897.

turn away to more fertile fields. The interest shows signs of exhaustion.

Students of philosophy will recognize what I mean when I say that this growing conviction of futility and consequent distaste are associated with the outcome of the famous dictum of Kant, that perception without conception is blind, while conception without perception is empty. The whole course of reflection since Kant's time has tended to justify this remark. The sensationalist and the rationalist have worked themselves out. Pretty much all students are convinced that we can reduce knowledge neither to a set of associated sensations, nor yet to a purely rational system of relations of thought. Knowledge is judgment, and judgment requires both a material of sense perception and an ordering, regulating principle, reason; so much seems certain, but we do not get any further. Sensation and thought themselves seem to stand out more rigidly opposed to each other in their own natures than ever. Why both are necessary, and how two such opposed factors coöperate in bringing about the unified result of science, becomes more and more of a mystery. It is the continual running up against this situation which accounts for the flagging of interest and the desire to direct energy where it will have more outcome.

This situation creates a condition favorable to taking stock of the question as it stands; to inquiring what this interest, prolonged for over three centuries, in the possibility and nature of knowledge, stands for; what the conviction as to the necessity of the union of sensation and thought, together with the inability to reach conclusions regarding the nature of the union, signifies.

I propose then to raise this evening precisely this question: What is the meaning of the problem of knowledge? What is its meaning, not simply for reflective philosophy or in terms of epistemology itself, but what is its meaning in the historical movement of humanity and as a part of a larger and more comprehensive experience? My thesis is perhaps sufficiently indicated in the mere taking of this point of view. It implies that the abstractness of the discussion of knowledge, its remoteness from everyday experience, is one of form, rather than of substance. It implies that the problem of knowledge is not a problem that has its origin, its value, or its destiny within itself. The problem is one which social life, the organized practice of mankind, has had to face. The seemingly technical and abstruse discussion of the philosophers results from the formulation and statement of the question.

I suggest that the problem of the possibility of knowledge is but an aspect of the question of the relation of knowing to acting, of theory to practice. The distinctions which the philosophers raise, the oppositions which they erect, the weary treadmill which they pursue between sensation and thought, subject and object, mind and matter, are not invented *ad hoc*, but are simply the concise reports and condensed formula of points of view and practical conflicts having their source in the very nature of modern life, conflicts which must be met and solved if modern life is to go on its way untroubled, with clear consciousness of what it is about. As the philosopher has received his problem from the world of action, so he must return his account there for auditing and liquidation.

More especially, I suggest that the tendency of all the points at issue to precipitate in the opposition of sensationalism and rationalism is due to the fact that sensation and reason stand for the two forces contending for mastery in social life: the radical and the conservative. The reason that the contest does not end, the reason for the necessity of the combination of the two in the resultant statement, is that both factors are necessary in action; one stands for stimulus, for initiative; the other for control, for direction.

I cannot hope, in the time at my command this evening, to justify these wide and sweeping assertions regarding either the origin, the work, or the final destiny of philosophic reflection. I simply hope, by reference to some of the chief periods of the development of philosophy, to illustrate to you something of what I mean.

At the outset we take a long scope in our survey and present to ourselves the epoch when philosophy was still consciously, and not simply by implication, human, when reflective thought had not developed its own technique of method, and was in no danger of being caught in its own machinery—the time of Socrates. What does the assertion of Socrates that an unexamined life is not one fit to be led by man; what does his injunction " Know thyself " mean? It means that the corporate motives and guarantees of conduct are breaking down. We have got away from the time when the individual could both regulate and justify his course of life by reference to the ideals incarnate in the habits of the community of which he is a member. The time of direct and therefore unconscious union with corporate life, finding therein stimuli, codes, and values, has departed. The development of industry and commerce, of war and politics, has brought face to face communities with different aims and diverse habits; the development of myth and animism into crude but genuine scientific observation and imagination has transformed the physical widening of the horizon, brought about by commerce and intercourse, into an intellectual and moral expansion. The old supports fail precisely at the time when they are most needed —before a widening and more complex scene of action. Where, then, shall the agent of action turn? The " Know thyself " of Socrates is the reply to the practical problem which confronted Athens in his day. Investigation into the true ends and worths of human life, sifting and testing of all competing ends, the discovery of a method which should validate the genuine and dismiss the spurious, had henceforth to do for man what consolidated and incorporate custom had hitherto presented as a free and precious gift.

With Socrates the question is as direct and practical as the question of making one's living or of governing the state; it is indeed the same question put in its general form. It is a question that the flute player, the cobbler, and the politician must face no more and no less than the reflective philosopher. The question is addressed by Socrates to every individual and to every group with which he comes in contact. Because the question is practical it is individual and direct. It is a question which every one must face and answer for himself, just as in the Protestant scheme every individual must face and solve for himself the question of his final destiny.

Yet the very attitude of Socrates carried with it the elements of its own destruction. Socrates could only raise the question, or rather demand of every individual that he raise it for himself. Of the answer he declared himself to be as ignorant as was any one. The result could be only a shifting of the center of interest. If the question is so all-important, and yet the wisest of all men must confess that he only knows his own ignorance as to its answer, the inevitable point of further consideration is the discovery of a method which shall enable the question to be answered. This is the significance of Plato. The problem is the absolutely inevitable outgrowth of the Socratic position; and yet it carried with it just as inevitably the separation of philosopher from shoemaker and statesman, and the relegation of theory to a position remote for the time being from conduct.

If the Socratic command, " Know thyself," runs against the dead wall of inability to conduct this knowledge, some one must take upon himself the discovery of how the requisite knowledge may be obtained. A new profession is born, that of the thinker. At this time the means, the discovery of how the aims and worths of the self may be known and measured, becomes, for this class, an end in itself. Theory is ultimately to be applied to practice; but in the meantime the theory must be worked out as theory or else no application. This represents the peculiar equilibrium and the peculiar point of contradiction in the Platonic system. All philosophy is simply for the sake of the organization and regulation of social life; and yet the philosophers must be a class by themselves, working out their peculiar problems with their own particular tools.

With Aristotle the attempted balance failed. Social life is disintegrating beyond the point of hope of a successful reorganization, and thinking is becoming a fascinating pursuit for its own sake. The world of practice is now the world of compromise and of adjustment. It is relative to partial aims and finite agents. The sphere of absolute and enduring truth and value can be reached only in and through thought. The one who acts compromises himself with the animal desire that inspires his action and with the alien material that forms its stuff. In two short generations the divorce of philosophy from life, the isolation of reflective theory from practical conduct, has completed itself. So great is the irony of history that this sudden and effective outcome was the result of the attempt to make thought the instrument of action, and action the manifestation of truth reached by thinking.

But this statement must not be taken too literally. It is impossible that men should really separate their ideas from their acts. If we look ahead a few centuries we find that the philosophy of Plato and Aristotle has accomplished, in an indirect and unconscious way, what perhaps it could never have effected by the more immediate and practical method of Socrates. Philosophy became an organ of vision, an instrument of interpretation; it furnished the medium through which the world was seen and the course of life estimated. Philosophy died as philosophy, to rise as the set and bent of the human mind. Through a thousand and devious and roundabout channels, the thoughts of the philosophers filtered through the strata of human consciousness and conduct. Through the teachings of grammarians, rhetoricians, and a variety of educational schools, they were spread in diluted form through the whole Roman Empire and were again precipitated in the common forms of speech. Through the earnestness of the moral propaganda of the Stoics they became the working rules of life for the more strenuous and earnest spirits. Through the speculations of the Sceptics and Epicureans they became the chief reliance and consolation of a large number of highly cultured individuals amid social turmoil and political disintegration. All these influences and many more finally summed themselves up in the two great media through which Greek philosophy finally fixed the intellectual horizon of man, determined the values of its perspective, and meted out the boundaries and divisions of the scene of human action.

These two influences were the development of Christian theology and moral theory, and the organization of the system of Roman jurisprudence.

There is perhaps no more fascinating chapter in the history of humanity than the slow and tortuous processes by which the ideas set in motion by that Athenian citizen who faced death as serenely as he conversed with a friend, finally became the intellectually organizing centers of the two great movements that bridge the span between ancient civilization and modern.   As the personal and immediate force and enthusiasm of the movement initiated by Jesus began to grow fainter and the commanding influence of his own personality commenced to dim, the ideas of the world and of life, of God and of man, elaborated in Greek philosophy, served to transform moral enthusiasm and personal devotion to the redemption of humanity, into a splendid and coherent view of the universe; a view that resisted all disintegrating influences and gathered into itself the permanent ideas and progressive ideals thus far developed in the history of man.

We have only a faint idea of how this was accomplished, or of the thoroughness of the work done. We have perhaps even more inadequate conceptions of the great organizing and centralizing work done by Greek thought in the political sphere. When the military and administrative genius of Rome brought the whole world in subjection to itself, the most pressing of practical problems was to give unity of practical aim and harmony of working machinery to the vast and confused mass of local custom and tradition, religious, social, economic, and intellectual, as well as political. In this juncture the great administrators and lawyers of Rome seized with avidity upon the results of the intellectual analysis of social and political relations elaborated in Greek philosophy. Caring naught for these results in their reflective and theoretical character, they saw in them the possible instrument of introducing order into chaos and of transforming the confused and conflicting medley of practice and opinion into a harmonious social structure. Roman law, that formed the vertebral column of civilization for a thousand years, and which articulated the outer order of life as distinctly as Christianity controlled the inner, was the outcome.

Thought was once more in unity with action, philosophy had become the instrument of conduct. Mr. Bosanquet makes the pregnant remark " that the weakness of medieval science and philosophy are connected rather with excess of practice than with excess of theory. The subordination of philosophy to theology is a subordination of science to a formulated conception of human welfare. Its essence is present, not wherever there is metaphysics but wherever the spirit of truth is subordinated to any preconceived practical intent." (" History of Esthetics," p. 146.)

Once more the irony of history displays itself. Thought has become practical, it has become the regulator of individual conduct and social organization, but at the expense of its own freedom and power. The defining characteristic of medievalism in state and in church, in political and spiritual life, is that truth presents itself to the individual only through the medium of organized authority.

There was a historical necessity on the external as well as the internal side. We have not the remotest way of imagining what the outcome would finally have been if, at the time when the intellectual structure of the Christian church and the legal structure of the Roman Empire had got themselves thoroughly organized, the barbarians had not made their inroads and seized upon all this accumulated and consolidated wealth as their own legitimate prey. But this was what did happen. As a result, truths originally developed by the freest possible criticism and investigation became external, and imposed themselves upon the mass of individuals by the mere weight of authoritative law. The external, transcendental, and supernatural character of spiritual truth and of social control during the Middle Ages is naught but the mirror, in consciousness, of the relation existing between the eager, greedy, undisciplined horde of barbarians on one side, and the concentrated achievements of ancient civilization on the other.

There was no way out save that the keen barbarian whet his appetite upon the rich banquet spread before him. But there was equally no way out so far as the continuity of civilization was concerned save that the very fullness and richness of this banquet set limits to the appetite, and finally, when assimilated and digested, it be transformed into the flesh and blood, the muscles and sinew of him who sat at the feast. Thus the barbarian ceased to be a barbarian and a new civilization arose.

But the time came when the work of absorption was fairly complete. The northern barbarians had eaten the food and drunk the wine of Græco-Roman civilization. The authoritative truth embodied in medieval state and church succeeded, in principle, in disciplining the untrained masses. Its very success issued its own death warrant. To say that it had succeeded means that the new people had finally eaten their way into the heart of the ideas offered them, had got from them what they wanted, and were henceforth prepared to go their own way and make their own living. Here a new rhythm of the movement of thought and action begins to show itself.

The beginning of this change in the swing of thought and action forms the transition from the Middle Ages to the modern times. It is the epoch of the Renaissance. The individual comes to a new birth and asserts his own individuality and demands his own rights in the way of feeling, doing, and knowing for himself. Science, art, religion, political life, must all be made over on the basis of recognizing the claims of the individual.

Pardon me these commonplaces, but they are necessary to the course of the argument. By historic fallacy we often suppose, or imagine that we suppose, that the individual had been present as a possible center of action all through the Middle Ages, but through some external and arbitrary interference had been weighted down by political and intellectual despotism. All this inverts the true order of the case. The very possibility of the individual making such unlimited demands for himself, claiming to be the legitimate center of all action and standard for all organization, was dependent, as I have already indicated, upon the intervening medievalism. Save as having passed through this period of tremendous discipline, and having gradually worked over into his own habits and purposes the truths embodied in the church and state that controlled his conduct, the individual could be only a source of disorder and a disturber of civilization. The very maintenance of the spiritual welfare of mankind was bound up in the extent to which the claim of truth and reality to be universal and objective, far above all individual feeling and thought, could make itself valid. The logical realism and universalism of scholastic

philosophy simply reflect the actual subjection of
the individual to that associated and corporate life
which, in conserving the past, provided the principle of control.

But the eager, hungry barbarian was there, implicated in this universalism. He must be active
in receiving and in absorbing the truth authoritatively doled out to him. Even the most rigid forms
of medieval Christianity could not avoid postulat-
ing the individual will as having a certain initiative
with reference to it' own salvation. The impulses,
the appetite, the instinct of the individual were all
assumed in medieval morals, religion, and politics.
The imagined medieval tyranny took them for
granted as completely as does the modern herald
of liberty and equality. But the medieval civilization knew that the time had not come when
these appetites and impulses could be trusted to
work themselves out. They must be controlled by
the incorporate truths inherited from Athens and
Rome.

The very logic of the relationship, however, required that the time come when the individual
makes his own the objective and universal truths.
He is now the incorporation of truth. He now has
the control as well as the stimulus of action within
himself. He is the standard and the end, as well
as the initiator and the effective force of execution.
Just because the authoritative truth of medieval-

ism has succeeded, has fulfilled its function, the individual can begin to assert himself.

Contrast this critical period, finding its expression equally in the art of the Renaissance, the revival of learning, the Protestant Reformation, and political democracy, with Athens in the time of Socrates. Then individuals felt their own social life disintegrated, dissolving under their very feet. The problem was how the value of that social life was to be maintained against the external and internal forces that were threatening it. The problem was on the side neither of the individual nor of progress; save as the individual was seen to be an intervening instrument in the reconstruction of the social unity. But with the individual of the fourteenth century, it was not his own intimate community life which was slipping away from him. It was an alien and remote life which had finally become his own; which had passed over into his own inner being. The problem was not how a unity of social life should be conserved, but what the individual should do with the wealth of resources of which he found himself the rightful heir and administrator. The problem looked out upon the future, not back to the past. It was how to create a new order, both of modes of individual conduct and forms of social life that should be the appropriate manifestations of the vigorous and richly endowed individual.

Hence the conception of progress as a ruling idea; the conception of the individual as the source and standard of rights; and the problem of knowledge, were all born together. Given the freed individual, who feels called upon to create a new heaven and a new earth, and who feels himself gifted with the power to perform the task to which he is called:—and the demand for science, for a method of discovering and verifying truth, becomes imperious. The individual is henceforth to supply control, law, and not simply stimulation and initiation. What does this mean but that instead of any longer receiving or assimilating truth, he is now to search for and create it? Having no longer the truth imposed by authority to rely upon, there is no resource save to secure the authority of truth. The possibility of getting at and utilizing this truth becomes therefore the underlying and conditioning problem of modern life. Strange as it may sound, the question which was formulated by Kant as that of the possibility of knowledge, is the fundamental political problem of modern life.

Science and metaphysics or philosophy, though seeming often to be at war, with their respective adherents often throwing jibes and slurs at each other, are really the most intimate allies. The philosophic movement is simply the coming to consciousness of this claim of the individual to be able to discover and verify truth for himself, and thereby not only to direct his own conduct, but to become an influential and decisive factor in the organization of life itself. Modern philosophy is the formulation of this creed, both in general and in its more specific implications. We often forget that the technical problem " *how* knowledge is possible," also means " how *knowledge* is possible "; how, that is, shall the individual be able to back himself up by truth which has no authority save that of its own intrinsic truthfulness. Science, on the other hand, is simply this general faith or creed asserting itself in detail; it is the practical faith at work engaged in subjugating the foreign territory of ignorance and falsehood step by step. If the ultimate outcome depends upon this detailed and concrete work, we must not forget that the earnestness and courage, as well as the intelligence and clearness with which the task has been undertaken, have depended largely upon the wider, even if vaguer, operation of philosophy.

But the student of philosophy knows more than that the problem of knowledge has been with increasing urgency and definiteness the persistent and comprehensive problem. So conscious is he of the two opposed theories regarding the nature of science, that he often forgets the underlying bond of unity of which we have been speaking. These two opposing schools are those which we know as the sensationalist and the intellectualist, the empiricist and the rationalist. Admitting that the dominance of the question of the possibility and nature of knowledge is at bottom a fundamental question of practice and of social direction, is *this* distinction anything more than the clash of scholastic opinions, a rivalry of ideas meaningless for conduct?

I think it is. Having made so many sweeping assertions I must venture one more. Fanciful and forced as it may seem, I would say that the sensational and empirical schools represent in conscious and reflective form the continuation of the principle of the northern and barbarian side of medieval life; while the intellectualist and the rationalist stand for the conscious elaboration of the principle involved in the Græco-Roman tradition.

Once more, as I cannot hope to prove, let me expand and illustrate. The sensationalist has staked himself upon the possibility of explaining and justifying knowledge by conceiving it as the grouping and combination of the qualities directly given us in sensation. The special reasons advanced in support of this position are sufficiently technical and remote. But the motive which has kept the sensationalist at work, which animated Hobbes and Locke, Hume and John Stuart Mill, Voltaire and Diderot, was a human not a scholastic one. It was the belief that only in sensation do we get any personal contact with reality, and hence, any genuine guarantee of vital truth. Thought is pale, and remote from the concrete stuff of knowledge and experience. It only formulates and duplicates; it only divides and recombines that fullness of vivid reality got directly and at first hand in sense experience. Reason, compared with sense, is indirect, emasculate, and faded.

Moreover, reason and thought in their very generality seem to lie beyond and outside the individual. In this remoteness, when they claim any final value, they violate the very first principle of the modern consciousness. What is the distinguishing characteristic of modern life, unless it be precisely that the individual shall not simply get, and reason about, truth in the abstract, but shall make it his own in the most intimate and personal way? He has not only to know the truth in the sense of knowing about it, but he must feel it. What is sensation but the answer to this demand for the most individual and intimate contact with reality? Show me a sensationalist and I will show you not only one who believes that he is on the side of concreteness and definiteness, as against washed-out abstractions and misty general notions: but also one who believes that he is identified with the cause of the individual as distinct from that of external authority. We have only to go to our Locke and our Mill to see that opposition to the innate and the *a priori* was felt to be opposition to the deification of hereditary prejudice and to the reception of ideas without examination or criticism. Personal contact with reality through sensation seemed to be the only safeguard from opinions which, while masquerading in the guise of absolute and eternal truth, were in reality but the prejudices of the past become so ingrained as to insist upon being standards of truth and action.

Positively as well as negatively, the sensationalists have felt themselves to represent the side of progress. In its supposed eternal character, a general notion stands ready made, fixed forever, without reference to time, without the possibility of change or diversity. As distinct from this, the sensation represents the never-failing eruption of the new. It is the novel, the unexpected, that which cannot be reasoned out in eternal formula, but must be hit upon in the ever-changing flow of our experience. It thus represents stimulation, excitation, momentum onwards. It gives a constant protest against the assumption of any theory or belief to possess finality; and it supplies the ever-renewed presentation of material out of which to build up new objects and new laws.

The sensationalist appears to have a good case. He stands for vividness and definiteness against abstraction; for the engagement of the individual in experience as against the remote and general

thought about experience; and for progress and
for variety against the eternal fixed monotony of
the concept. But what says the rationalist?
What value has experience, he inquires, if it is simply a chaos of disintegrated and floating débris?
What is the worth of personality and individuality
when they are reduced to crudity of brute feeling
and sheer intensity of impulsive reaction? What
is there left in progress that we should desire it,
when it has become a mere unregulated flux of
transitory sensations, coming and going without
reasonable motivation or rational purpose?

Thus the intellectualist has endeavored to frame
the structure of knowledge as a well-ordered economy, where reason is sovereign, where the permanent is the standard of reference for the changing,
and where the individual may always escape from
his own mere individuality and find support and
reinforcement in a system of relations that lies
outside of and yet gives validity to his own passing
states of consciousness. Thus the rationalists hold
that we must find in a universal intelligence a
source of truth and guarantee of value that is
sought in vain in the confused and flowing mass
of sensations.

The rationalist, in making the concept or general idea the all-important thing in knowledge, believes himself to be asserting the interests of order
as against destructive caprice and the license of

momentary whim. He finds that his cause is bound up with that of the discovery of truth as the necessary instrument and method for action. Only by reference to the general and the rational can the individual find perspective, secure direction for his appetites and impulses, and escape from the uncontrolled and ruinous reactions of his own immediate tendency.

The concept, once more, in its very generality, in its elevation above the intensities and conflicts of momentary passions and interests, is the conserver of the experience of the past. It is the wisdom of the past put into capitalized and funded form to enable the individual to get away from the stress and competition of the needs of the passing moment. It marks the difference between barbarism and civilization, between continuity and disintegration, between the sequence of tradition that is the necessity of intelligent thought and action, and the random and confused excitation of the hour.

When we thus consider not the details of the positions of the sensationalist and rationalist, but the motives that have induced them to assume these positions, we discover what is meant in saying that the question is still a practical, a social one, and that the two schools stand for certain one-sided factors of social life. If we have on one side the demand for freedom, for personal initiation into experience, for variety and progress, we have on the other side the demand for general order, for continuous and organized unity, for the conservation of the dearly bought resources of the past. This is what I mean by saying that the sensationalist abstracts in conscious form the position and tendency of the Germanic element in modern civilization, the factor of appetite and impulse, of keen enjoyment and satisfaction, of stimulus and initiative. Just so the rationalist erects into conscious abstraction the principle of the Græco-Roman world, that of control, of system, of order and authority.

That the principles of freedom and order, of past and future, or conservation and progress, of incitement to action and control of that incitation, are correlative, I shall not stop to argue. It may be worth while, however, to point out that exactly the same correlative and mutually implicating connection exists between sensationalism and rationalism, considered as philosophical accounts of the origin and nature of knowledge.

The strength of each school lies in the weakness of its opponent. The more the sensationalist appears to succeed in reducing knowledge to the associations of sensation, the more he creates a demand for thought to introduce background and relationship. The more consistent the sensationalist, the more openly he reveals the sensation in its own nakedness crying aloud for a clothing of value and meaning which must be borrowed from reflective and rational interpretation. On the other hand, the more reason and the system of relations that make up the functioning of reason are magnified, the more is felt the need of sensation to bring reason into some fruitful contact with the materials of experience. Reason must have the stimulus of this contact in order to be incited to its work and to get materials to operate with. The cause, then, why neither school can come to rest in itself is precisely that each abstracts one essential factor of conduct.

This suggests, finally, that the next move in philosophy is precisely to transfer attention from the details of the position assumed, and the arguments used in these two schools, to the practical motives that have unconsciously controlled the discussion. The positions have been sufficiently elaborated. Within the past one hundred years, within especially the last generation, each has succeeded in fully stating its case. The result, if we remain at this point, is practically a deadlock. Each can make out its case against the other. To stop at such a point is a patent absurdity. If we are to get out of the cul-de-sac it must be by bringing into consciousness the tacit reference to action that all the time has been the controlling factor.

In a word, another great rhythmic movement is seen to be approaching its end. The demand for science and philosophy was the demand for truth and a sure standard of truth which the new-born individual might employ in his efforts to build up a new world to afford free scope to the powers stirring within him. The urgency and acuteness of this demand caused, for the time being, the transfer of attention from the nature of practice to that of knowledge. The highly theoretical and abstract character of modern epistemology, combined with the fact that this highly abstract and theoretic problem has continuously engaged the attention of thought for more than three centuries, is, to my mind, proof positive that the question of knowledge was for the time being the point in which the question of practice centered, and through which it must find outlet and solution.

We return, then, to our opening problem: the meaning of the question of the possibility of knowledge raised by Kant a century ago, and of his assertion that sensation without thought is blind, thought without sensation empty. Once more I recall to the student of philosophy how this assertion of Kant has haunted and determined the course of philosophy in the intervening years—how his solution at once seems inevitable and unsatisfactory. It is inevitable in that no one can fairly deny that both sense and reason are implicated in every fruitful and significant statement of the world; unconvincing because we are after all left with these two opposed things still at war with each other, plus the miracle of their final combination.

When I say that the only way out is to place the whole modern industry of epistemology in relation to the conditions that gave it birth and the function it has to fulfil, I mean that the unsatisfactory character of the entire neo-Kantian movement lies in its assumption that knowledge gives birth to itself and is capable of affording its own justification. The solution that is always sought and never found so long as we deal with knowledge as a self-sufficing purveyor of reality, reveals itself when we conceive of knowledge as a statement of action, that statement being necessary, moreover, to the successful ongoing of action.

The entire problem of medieval philosophy is that of absorption, of assimilation. The result was the creation of the individual. Hence the problem of modern life is that of reconstruction, reform, reorganization. The entire content of experience needs to be passed through the alembic of individual agency and realization. The individual is to be the bearer of civilization; but this involves a remaking of the civilization that he bears. Thus we have the dual question: How can the individual become the organ of corporate action? How can he make over the truth authoritatively embodied in institutions of church and state into frank, healthy, and direct expressions of the simple act of free living? On the other hand, how can civilization preserve its own integral value and import when subordinated to the agency of the individual instead of exercising supreme sway over him?

The question of knowledge, of the discovery and statement of truth, gives the answer to this question; and it alone gives the answer. Admitting that the practical problem of modern life is the maintenance of the moral values of civilization through the medium of the insight and decision of the individual, the problem is foredoomed to futile failure save as the individual in performing his task can work with a definite and controllable tool. This tool is science. But this very fact, constituting the dignity of science and measuring the importance of the philosophic theory of knowledge, conferring upon them the religious value once attaching to dogma and the disciplinary significance once belonging to political rules, also sets their limit. The servant is not above his master.

When a theory of knowledge forgets that its value rests in solving the problem out of which it has arisen, viz., that of securing a method of action; when it forgets that it has to work out the conditions under which the individual may freely direct himself without loss to the historic values of civilization—when it forgets these things it begins to cumber the ground. It is a luxury, and hence a social nuisance and disturber. Of course, in the very nature of things, every means or instrument will for a while absorb attention so that it becomes the end. Indeed it is the end when it is an indispensable condition of onward movement. But when once the means have been worked out they must operate as such. When the nature and method of knowledge are fairly understood, then interest must transfer itself from the possibility of knowledge to the possibility of its application to life.

The sensationalist has played his part in bringing to effective recognition the demand in valid knowledge for individuality of experience, for personal participation in materials of knowledge. The rationalist has served his time in making it clear once for all that valid knowledge requires organization, and the operation of a relatively permanent and general factor. The Kantian epistemologist has formulated the claims of both schools in defining judgment as the relation of perception and conception. But when it goes on to state that this relation is itself knowledge, or can be found in knowledge, it stultifies itself. Knowledge can define the percept and elaborate the concept, but their union can be found only in action. The experimental method of modern science, its erection into the ultimate mode of verification, is simply this

fact obtaining recognition. Only action can reconcile the old, the general, and the permanent with
the changing, the individual, and the new. It is
action as progress, as development, making over
the wealth of the past into capital with which to
do an enlarging and freer business, that alone can
find its way out of the cul-de-sac of the theory of
knowledge. Each of the older movements passed
away because of its own success, failed because it
did its work, died in accomplishing its purpose.
So also with the modern philosophy of knowledge;
there must come a time when we have so much
knowledge in detail, and understand so well its
method in general, that it ceases to be a problem.
It becomes a tool. If the problem of knowledge
is not intrinsically meaningless and absurd it must
in course of time be solved. Then the dominating
interest becomes the *use* of knowledge; the conditions under which and ways in which it may be
most organically and effectively employed to direct
conduct.

Thus the Socratic period recurs; but recurs with
the deepened meaning of the intervening weary
years of struggle, confusion, and conflict in the
growth of the recognition of the need of patient
and specific methods of interrogation. So, too, the
authoritative and institutional truth of scholasti-
cism recurs, but recurs borne up upon the vigorous
and conscious shoulders of the freed individual who

is aware of his own intrinsic relations to truth, and who glories in his ability to carry civilization —not merely to carry it, but to carry it on. Thus another swing in the rhythm of theory and practice begins.

How does this concern us as philosophers? For the world it means that philosophy is henceforth a method and not an original fountain head of truth, nor an ultimate standard of reference. But what is involved for philosophy itself in this change? I make no claims to being a prophet, but I venture one more and final unproved statement, believing, with all my heart, that it is justified both by the moving logic of the situation, and by the signs of the times. I refer to the growing transfer of interest from metaphysics and the theory of knowledge to psychology and social ethics— including in the latter term all the related concrete social sciences, so far as they may give guidance to conduct.

There are those who see in psychology only a particular science which they are pleased to term purely empirical (unless it happen to restate in changed phraseology the metaphysics with which they are familiar). They see in it only a more or less incoherent mass of facts, interesting because relating to human nature, but below the natural sciences in point of certainty and definiteness, as also far below pure philosophy as to con.prehensiveness and ability to deal with fundamental issues. But if I may be permitted to dramatize a little the position of the psychologist, he can well afford to continue patiently at work, unmindful of the occasional supercilious sneers of the epistemologist. The cause of modern civilization stands and falls with the ability of the individual to serve as its agent and bearer. And psychology is naught but the account of the way in which individual life is thus progressively maintained and reorganized. Psychology is the attempt to state in detail the machinery of the individual considered as the instrument and organ through which social action operates. It is the answer to Kant's demand for the formal phase of experience—how experience as such is constituted. Just because the whole burden and stress, both of conserving and advancing experience is more and more thrown upon the individual, everything which sheds light upon how the individual may weather the stress and assume the burden is precious and imperious.

Social ethics in inclusive sense is the correlative science. Dealing not with the form or mode or machinery of action, it attempts rather to make out its filling and make up the values that are necessary to constitute an experience which is worth while. The sociologist, like the psychologist, often presents himself as a camp follower of genuine science and philosophy, picking up scraps here and there and piecing them together in somewhat of an aimless fashion—fortunate indeed, if not vague and over-ambitious. Yet social ethics represents the attempt to translate philosophy from a general and therefore abstract method into a working and specific method; it is the change from inquiring into the nature of value in general to inquiring as to the *particular* values that ought to be realized in the life of every one, and as to the conditions which render possible this realization.

There are those who will see in this conception of the outcome of a four-hundred-year discussion concerning the nature and possibility of knowledge a derogation from the high estate of philosophy. There are others who will see in it a sign that philosophy, after wandering aimlessly hither and yon in a wilderness without purpose or outcome, has finally come to its senses—has given up metaphysical absurdities and unverifiable speculations, and become a purely positive science of phenomena. But there are yet others who will see in this movement the fulfilment of its vocation, the clear consciousness of a function that it has always striven to perform; and who will welcome it as a justification of the long centuries when it appeared to sit apart, far from the common concerns of man, busied with discourse of essence and cause, absorbed in argument concerning subject and object, reason and sensation.   To such this outcome will appear the inevitable sequel of the saying of Socrates that " an unexamined life is not one fit to be led by man "; and a better response to his injunction "Know thyself."

THE END

INDEX

INDEX

GREAT BOOKS IN PHILOSOPHY PAPERBACK SERIES

ETHICS

Aristotle—*The Nicomachean Ethics*	$8.95
Marcus Aurelius—*Meditations*	5.95
Jeremy Bentham—*The Principles of Morals and Legislation*	8.95
John Dewey—*The Moral Writings of John Dewey, Revised Edition* (edited by James Gouinlock)	10.95
Epictetus—*Enchiridion*	3.95
Immanuel Kant—*Fundamental Principles of the Metaphysic of Morals*	4.95
John Stuart Mill—*Utilitarianism*	4.95
George Edward Moore—*Principia Ethica*	8.95
Friedrich Nietzsche—*Beyond Good and Evil*	8.95
Plato—*Protagoras, Philebus,* and *Gorgias*	7.95
Bertrand Russell—*Bertrand Russell On Ethics, Sex, and Marriage* (edited by Al Seckel)	19.95
Arthur Schopenhauer—*The Wisdom of Life* and *Counsels and Maxims*	6.95
Benedict de Spinoza—*Ethics* and *The Improvement of the Understanding*	9.95

SOCIAL AND POLITICAL PHILOSOPHY

Aristotle—*The Politics*	7.95
Francis Bacon—*Essays*	6.95
Mikhail Bakunin—*The Basic Bakunin: Writings, 1869–1871* (translated and edited by Robert M. Cutler)	10.95
Edmund Burke—*Reflections on the Revolution in France*	7.95
John Dewey—*Freedom and Culture*	10.95
G. W. F. Hegel—*The Philosophy of History*	9.95
Thomas Hobbes—*The Leviathan*	7.95
Sidney Hook—*Paradoxes of Freedom*	9.95
Sidney Hook—*Reason, Social Myths, and Democracy*	11.95
John Locke—*Second Treatise on Civil Government*	4.95
Niccolo Machiavelli—*The Prince*	4.95
Karl Marx—*The Poverty of Philosophy*	7.95
Karl Marx/Frederick Engels—*The Economic and Philosophic Manuscripts of 1844* and *The Communist Manifesto*	6.95
John Stuart Mill—*Considerations on Representative Government*	6.95
John Stuart Mill—*On Liberty*	4.95
John Stuart Mill—*On Socialism*	7.95
John Stuart Mill—*The Subjection of Women*	4.95
Friedrich Nietzsche—*Thus Spake Zarathustra*	9.95
Thomas Paine—*Common Sense*	5.95
Thomas Paine—*Rights of Man*	7.95
Plato—*Lysis, Phaedrus,* and *Symposium*	6.95
Plato—*The Republic*	9.95
Jean-Jacques Rousseau—*The Social Contract*	5.95
Mary Wollstonecraft—*A Vindication of the Rights of Men*	4.95
Mary Wollstonecraft—*A Vindication of the Rights of Women*	6.95

METAPHYSICS/EPISTEMOLOGY

Aristotle—*De Anima*	6.95
Aristotle—*The Metaphysics*	9.95
George Berkeley—*Three Dialogues Between Hylas and Philonous*	4.95
René Descartes—*Discourse on Method* and *The Meditations*	6.95
John Dewey—*How We Think*	10.95
John Dewey—*The Influence of Darwin on Philosophy and Other Essays*	11.95
Epicurus—*The Essential Epicurus: Letters, Principal Doctrines, Vatican Sayings, and Fragments*	
(translated, and with an introduction, by Eugene O'Connor)	5.95
Sidney Hook—*The Quest for Being*	11.95
David Hume—*An Enquiry Concerning Human Understanding*	4.95
David Hume—*Treatise of Human Nature*	9.95
William James—*The Meaning of Truth*	11.95
William James—*Pragmatism*	7.95
Immanuel Kant—*Critique of Practical Reason*	7.95
Immanuel Kant—*Critique of Pure Reason*	9.95
Gottfried Wilhelm Leibniz—*Discourse on Method* and the *Monadology*	6.95
John Locke—*An Essay Concerning Human Understanding*	9.95
Plato—*The Euthyphro, Apology, Crito, and Phaedo*	5.95
Bertrand Russell—*The Problems of Philosophy*	8.95
Sextus Empiricus—*Outlines of Pyrrhonism*	8.95

PHILOSOPHY OF RELIGION

Ludwig Feuerbach—*The Essence of Christianity*	8.95
David Hume—*Dialogues Concerning Natural Religion*	5.95
John Locke—*A Letter Concerning Toleration*	4.95
Thomas Paine—*The Age of Reason*	13.95
Bertrand Russell—*Bertrand Russell On God and Religion* (edited by Al Seckel)	19.95

ESTHETICS

Aristotle—*The Poetics*	5.95
Aristotle—*Treatise on Rhetoric*	7.95

GREAT MINDS PAPERBACK SERIES

ECONOMICS

Charlotte Perkins Gilman—*Women and Economics: A Study of the Economic Relation between Women and Men*	11.95
John Maynard Keynes—*The General Theory of Employment, Interest, and Money*	11.95
Alfred Marshall—*Principles of Economics*	11.95
David Ricardo—*Principles of Political Economy and Taxation*	10.95
Adam Smith—*Wealth of Nations*	9.95

RELIGION

Thomas Henry Huxley—*Agnosticism and Christianity and Other Essays*	10.95
Ernest Renan—*The Life of Jesus*	11.95
Voltaire—*A Treatise on Toleration and Other Essays*	8.95
Andrew D. White—*A History of the Warfare of Science with Theology in Christendom*	19.95

SCIENCE

HISTORY

SOCIOLOGY

CRITICAL ESSAYS

(Prices subject to change without notice.)

ORDER FORM

Prometheus Books
59 John Glenn Drive • Amherst, New York 14228–2197
Telephone: (716) 691–0133

Phone Orders (24 hours):
Toll free (800) 421–0351 • FAX (716) 691–0137
Email: PBooks6205@aol.com

Ship to: _____

Address _____

_____

City _____

County (*N.Y. State Only*) _____

Telephone _____

Prometheus Acct. # _____

❑ Payment enclosed (or)

Charge to ❑ VISA ❑ MasterCard

A/C: ☐☐☐☐☐☐☐☐☐☐☐☐☐☐☐☐☐☐☐☐

Exp. Date _____ / _____

Signature _____